Storytel...

Contents

What Are Storytellers?

"Ha ma wa." That means
"a long time ago".

A long time ago, people
began to make Storytellers.
A Storyteller is a clay figure.

Usually it is talking or singing.
Usually it has little figures
sitting on its lap.

Telling stories is a way
for people to share information.

It is a way for old people
to teach young people.

Storytellers help people
to remember their stories.

Where Do Storytellers Come From?

Helen Cordero is the most famous Storyteller maker.

She was born in 1915 at the Cochiti Pueblo in New Mexico.

She started making clay figures because making pots was too hard.

She remembered how
children loved hearing her
grandfather tell stories.

She made figures.
She covered them
with little children.

She called these figures
"Storytellers".

This turtle
Storyteller was
made by
Buffy Cordero,
granddaughter of
Helen Cordero.

More and more people
started to make Storytellers.

Today, the word "Storyteller"
means any figure
that is covered with
children or baby animals.

Some artists make animals covered with baby animals.

Some artists make people covered with children.

Animal Storytellers

Many Storyteller figures are different animals.

Most of the animals
learn a lesson in their story.

Then the animal becomes
the Storyteller.
It can tell the story
to the little ones.

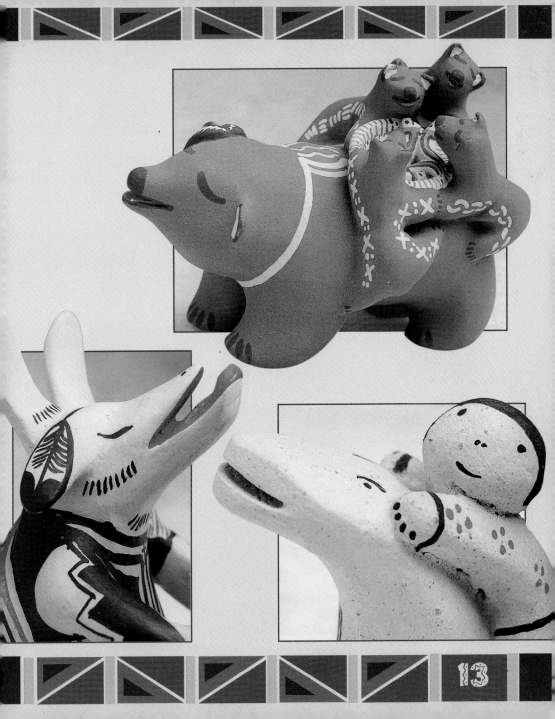

Patterns in Storytellers

The designs in Storytellers
tell a story, too.

Sometimes a pattern
has a special meaning.

Sometimes a pattern is
a sign for a group or family.

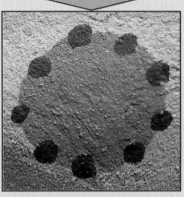

Find this pattern.

Storyteller

Artists pass on their special patterns to their children, just like the Storytellers pass on their stories.

Storytellers with Drums

Many Storytellers have drums.

Drums help people remember
the rhythm of the stories.

Each beat makes a pattern
that can be chanted.

Chanting is a good way
to remember something.

You Can Make a Storyteller

To make a Storyteller,
you will need clay or salt dough.

1. Make a round body.
   Add a head.

2. Roll out arms and legs.
Put them on the body.

3. Make some little babies.
Put them all over the figure.

4. When your Storyteller is dry,
decorate it with paints.
Put your special "mark"
on your Storyteller.

You Can Tell a Story

Think of a story
that is special to you.
Start your story with
"Ha ma wa".
Tell your story to a friend.

The Bear and the Snakes

told by Kate, age 8

Ha ma wa, a bear was sleeping in his den. Some snakes came slithering into his den to get warm. The bear was so warm and furry, the snakes coiled tighter and tighter around the bear's body. Then the bear woke up!

He scolded the snakes and kicked them out of his den. "Let that be a lesson!" he said. "If you squeeze too tight, you'll sleep outside at night."

Salt Dough Recipe

2 cups flour
1 cup salt
1 cup water

1. Mix flour, salt, and water.

2. Knead dough into a soft ball.

3. Add more flour or water as needed.

4. Form figure.

5. Air dry, or bake at 350°F (180°C) for 15 – 20 minutes.

Grand Designs

In the summer of 2015, our Year 7 students embarked on our 'Grand Designs' learning expedition to investigate 'What in nature inspires us?' and 'Is there a design to nature?'

We started the expedition by looking at cave art, which got us thinking about how man has been inspired by nature from as far back as history is able to tell us, and spent time in sites of natural beauty such as Sandall Beat Wood so that we too could be similarly inspired.

During the first case study we read 'The Voyage of the Beagle' and learned about the massive impact that Darwin's theories had on the highly religious Victorian British society.

Just as Darwin did on the Beagle, we kept a scientific journal, recording stories from our fieldwork, as well as notes and sketches about the many areas of the curriculum we studied.

We discovered how mathematical ratios and sequences such as the Fibonacci numbers are found throughout nature and learned how to express sequences algebraically and how to manipulate ratios.

In the second case study, we spent a day a week at Potteric Carr, with our expert Kat Wooley, helping to build the paths and fire pits in the new Bostow Plantation area. Kat also told us where to find our species at Potteric so that we could observe their behaviour before writing about them.

To aid with our writing, we studied the animal poems of Ted Hughes and used similar linguistic techniques in our first person narratives to bring our animals to life on the page, alongside a scientific description of their adaptations, habitat and place in the food web.

Finally, we created scientifically accurate, multi-colour prints from lino to complete the work included in this book.

We hope you find this field guide both purposeful and beautiful.

XP.

Robin

The sun is piercing through the woodland's skyline, the branches twisted, as faces appeared in the moss covered trees. Crunchy twigs cover the ground like a blanket and the mud like a thick dark soup of dirt carpeted the woodland.

I can see the shimmering sun glistening into my eyes as I elegantly soar through the beautiful summer's sky. I taste the freedom of being able to go wherever I want. I hear the world spinning as I glide through the air. I smell the freshly cut grass as I hover over the open, fresh fields. I touch the river's surface as I elegantly skim its surface.

I stood on the grass plains digging for worms. I pulled one out of the ground, it stretched like an elastic band as I tugged at it with force. It popped out. I gulped it down in one. I pinched a ripe red berry off a bright green tree and ate it a bit at a time. I fly back to my nest to look after my eggs and to keep them warm.

Facts

Common name: Robin
Scientific name: Erithacus rubecula
Status: Least concern
Size: Weight 22g. Wingspan 20-22cm. Length 13-14cm.

Adaptations
You can identify a robin by their bright red chest and white neck. It loves to fly near water and in woodlands. You might be surprised to find that the small creatures can be very protective and will fight over their territories. Its song is high pitched and sounds like a chirping sound and the phrases are long.

Habitat
The robin lives in woodland nests high up in trees and in wetland such as ponds and rivers. They often go near bird feeders. When they are out they often stay in between the trees. You will find robins mostly near Willow Pool Hide.

Interdependence
The robin is an omnivore because it eats worms and berries and it is eaten by owls. It is a primary and secondary consumer because it eats berries which are producers, but it also eats worms which are primary consumers.

Did you know?
The robin's red breast is often associated with fire because of the colour and how aggressive they can be.

Song Thrush

My home is filled with jewels. Green grass, the colour of emeralds, the sky as blue as sapphires and ruby red roses surround me, lining my eyes with bright colours. Meanwhile, my ears are occupied by the soft, sweet songs of other birds and the strong smell of pollen. I weave through the tall trees and dancing blades of grass. With every step my feathers are gently stroked by the grass and flowers.

I hear a strange but almost familiar noise nearby. I look up and see a hawk gliding through the sky like a deadly stringless kite. I panic wondering whether this is my end. What can I do? I have to act quickly because it might have not seen me yet. I dive behind a tree hoping to stay off its radar. I hop out into the open, checking if its still there. That was a mistake, I am now in its eye line. There is a slim chance of me leaving this situation alive. I look beside me and see a rabbit who is larger and slower than me. Perhaps this is my chance to escape. The hawk is now focusing on the bigger prey, so I take the chance and escape my near death.

As I glance back the hawk dives down to the unfortunate rabbit. So I fly swiftly, relieved to be safe. I fly through the air, my wings flapping rapidly, while scanning the ground for my home and checking I am not being followed. Finally I find it. I swoop down for the last time today and settle in my nest. I am safe.

Facts

Common name: Song Thrush
Scientific name: Turdus philomelos
Status: Least concern
Size: Length 23cm. Wingspan 33-36cm. Weight 70-90g.

Adaptations
Male song thrushes have brown wings, and a white breast speckled with brown. The song thrushes have adapted behaviourally to move away when the weather is cold, because they are not immune to the cold. They have also adapted to live in woodland areas to find more food and have a safe environment.

Habitat
In Britain they are found in many places such as gardens, thickets, hedges, copses and woods. They are frequently found in suburban areas. At Potteric Carr Nature Reserve, they are found in St Catherine's Copse, Beeston Plantation and Loversall Carr.

Interdependence
The song thrush is a secondary consumer. Its main diet is worms which is the primary consumer and the worms feed on grass which is the producer.

Did you know?
The generic name, Turdus, is the Latin for thrush. Philomelos refers to a character in Greek mythology, Philomela, who had her tongue cut out, but was changed into a singing bird.

Little Grebe

The sweet sound of birds singing awakes me from my sleep. I feel the scorching sun as it increasingly heats my small body. Stretching out wide from the warm spot that I slept in, I waddled down to the water's edge. I watch the smooth ripple of the lake's current as it brushes against my feet. Launching myself into ice cold water like a torpedo exiting a submarine, I see the reeds wave at me, wind rushing through them, hearing the rustle of the reeds like someone blowing aggressively.

Bobbing up and down like a buoy on the unsettled sea, gliding out through a gateway of vivid colours: blues, pinks, creams and greens. Swiftly coasting around the wonderland of a lake shaded by the lush green trees that surround the lake like a frame. Brushing my feathers against the soft alabaster reeds. Aggravating all of the other animals on the water, by making a loud whining noise. I retreat back to shore as I see a flock of agitated birds heading straight for me.

Facts

Common name: Little Grebe
Scientific name: Tachybaptus ruficollis
Status: Moderate concern
Size: 25-29cm, weight up to 140g

Adaptations
The little grebe is a small water bird with a pointed bill. In summer, the little grebe is easy to spot with its rich reddish brown coloured neck, cheeks and flanks. They have large lobed feet instead of webbed feet; these help them to swim in water and walk on soft, slippery ground such as mud flats or reed beds. One way to identify the little grebe is to look out for the tail which appears like a small fluffy tuft.

Habitat
The little grebe inhabits a wide range of small and shallow wetlands usually less than 1m deep, with lots of rich vegetation. Suitable habitats include small lakes, ponds, sheltered bays and vegetated shores of larger freshwater, just like the many lakes found in Potteric Carr.

Interdependence
The little grebe is an omnivore meaning it eats other animals and vegetation. The little grebe is part of a food chain where is acts as a secondary consumer by eating insects, or as tertiary consumer by eating small fish. Little grebes can fall prey to foxes. Foxes are an example of an apex predator which have no natural predators and are top of the food chain.

Did you know?
The little grebe can hide submerged (go fully underwater) when frightened, and can dive for up to 40 seconds under the water before they have to come back up for air.

Blue Tit

I hopped delicately on the hard ground. Then, as I leap into the sky to fly, I see graceful birds fluttering through the sunset, creating a beautiful silhouette. Then, as I fly through the sky a sparrowhawk starts to chase me.

As I fly from tree to tree, I hear other birds tweeting. As the sun shines on my tree, I suddenly feel hot, so I go and get a drink to cool myself down. As I pass through the garden on this single hot sunny day, I eat insects, caterpillars, seeds, and nuts. After I eat, my tummy feels full, so I fly up and hide in my tree.

Facts

Common name: Blue Tit
Scientific name: Cyanistes caeruleus
Status: Least concern
Size: Weight 11g. Wingspan 12-14cm. Length 12cm.

Adaptations
The blue tit is green and blue at the side of the body. They have a blue tail and wings, and a white head. They have blue caps on their eyes with a black strip over them, and they have a blue chin. They have got feathers to keep warm, and wings to fly and catch insects. Their beaks are very small, strong and stubby, because they need to open nuts and seeds to eat them. They are well-adapted to looking out for predators. They listen out for distress calls from other birds. They recognise this as a warning and then fly away.

Habitat
Blue tits are found in many habitats types throughout the UK such as woodlands, parks, gardens, farmland, hedgerows. They can often be seen in the wooded areas in Potteric Carr such as in the trees around Willow marsh.

Interdependence
Blue tits eat insects, nuts and seeds. This means that they are omnivores, which means that they eat producers and consumers.

Did you know?
Blue tits are common garden birds and can be seen all year round if you look out for them.

Canada Goose

Morning approaches and as the sky lightens, the lake glistens like thousands of tiny stars, as the sunrise hides them away. The afterglow of the night illuminates the sky with vibrant shades of orange and pink. As the sky is painted, the wetlands brighten with different colours and the sun rises slowly from the sky.

I waddle over to the marshy, reedy lake and honk in annoyance as my webbed feet skate out from under me and I slide across the cool, icy surface. As I thrust my beak into the frozen lake it shatters, splitting with a great crack straight through the middle. The ice shrieks in a great piercing cry. As a small puddle of water splashed up over the ice in small waves, dominating it with a millimetre thick layer of water. I lap at it thirstily. Strutting across the hard slippery surface, I hear the faint noise of birdsong. Whilst the noise grows louder, I glance around and see three black headed gulls skating across the ice, fear and annoyance clear in their eyes. After watching them comically skate around for a while I fly off, back to the nest.

Morning approaches and as the sky lightens the lake glistens like thousands of tiny stars as the sunrise hides them away. The afterglow of the night sky illuminates with orange and pink. As the sky is painted, the wetlands brighten with different colours and the sun rises slowly from the sky.

As the beautiful lake starts to awake from a deep slumber, I smile to myself, knowing that the same beauty will come again tomorrow.

Facts

Common name: Canada Goose
Scientific name: Branta canadensis
Status: Least concern
Size: Wingspan 127-185cm. Length 75-110cm.

Adaptations
Canada geese have some behavioural adaptations such as migration in populations of North America, and flying in a V formation which helps save energy when flying for a long time. Canada geese have a long wingspan which helps them to migrate thousands of miles from Canada to the US. European populations are mostly non-migratory as the climate is more stable here due to the gulf stream. They also have webbed feet for swimming and a billed beak, which helps it to pluck grass from the marshes. Canada geese are social birds and like to travel in flocks and you may often hear them making a distinctive 'honking' or 'barking' sound as they fly overhead.

Habitat
You can see Canada geese in Britain all year round, though they can move from place to place. They were introduced to Europe hundreds of years ago. Canada geese like wetlands because they eat the grasses produced there. In Potteric Carr, they can be found at Decoy Marsh or around Willow Marsh.

Interdependence
The Canada goose is on the second trophic level and is a primary consumer. They eat grass which is the producer, making them herbivores, though may eat insects from time to time. They may also be eaten by foxes who are apex predators.

Did you know?
Another term for a group of geese is a 'flock', a 'gaggle' or a 'nide'. When flying they are called a 'wedge' or 'skein' of geese.

Little Ringed Plover

As I glide through the sky, I feel the wind running through my feathers. I feel a breeze moving over me and the cold, thin air makes me shiver. I spot a worm below, and I dive. I scoop it up with my talons and take it to the nearest tree. I start to repeatedly peck at it. Slowly, my prey succombs, until eventually I swallow it. I stop for a minute. I feel the sun's rays shining on me, as I listen to the other bird song. Their calls are beautiful, chirping and singing like a chorus of angels.

I preen my feathers and get ready to fly. I flap my wings and join my flock. We glide through the sky in group formation, staying together until we land in the wetlands. I look for insects on the ground, but none can be seen. I am still hungry; the flight was exhausting. I decide to fly back to my nest. As make my way back, I suddenly feel under observation. Is a predator watching me, or am I just paranoid? But no, I hear the squawk of a sparrowhawk and I see the ravenous bird diving from above. I start to flap my wings ferociously in panic, like a mouse being chased by an agile cat. I can see my nest from here, I am so close. I put in every last bit of energy to get there. The bird is close on my tail. I'm not giving up, 'I will get there' I think to myself. I get to my tree and, luckily for me, the bird can't fit through the branches, I am safe. I shakily sit in my nest; slowly retrieving my energy. I see the sparrowhawk circling the tree above me, still in pursuit, but eventually he gives up and flies off. I eat some berries that I had saved, and decide to get some rest and see what the next day brings.

Facts

Common name: Little Ringed Plover
Scientific name: Charadrius dubius
Status: Least concern
Size: Wingspan 45cm. Length 14cm. Weight 40g.

Adaptations
You can identify the little ringed plover from its curved beak, adapted for getting into snail shells. It has brown wings and a white body, with a grey patch on the top of its head and a black and orange ringed eye. It also has a black ring of feathers around its neck.

Habitat
You will find the little ringed plover on the ground most of the time; it is independent so is normally found alone and not in numbers. You can find the little ringed plover on flats. It migrates from Europe, Asia and Africa in spring and leaves in autumn. It is seen most between March and October. You will see them on grass flats and wetlands. At Potteric Carr, they are most likely to be seen on Willow Marsh and Decoy Marsh.

Interdependence
The little ringed plover is a carnivore. It eats things like worms, snails and insects. This means it is a tertiary consumer. It is not an apex predator because it is eaten by species such as sparrowhawks on occasion.

Did you know?
Did you know that the little ringed plover was first bred in the UK in 1938.

Wood Pigeon

It was a warm summer's morning, the sun rose and I woke feeling very hungry. The air was fresh and clear like the water from a high mountain spring. I was waiting for the human to put some food on the bird table. After waiting for a couple of hours, the human finally put some food out, then went away. I lay on my tummy and nibbled the crumbs, they fell out of my beak but it did not distract me from my gorging.

After a lovely breakfast, I flew off flapping my wings, then gliding, then flying. I was cutting through the air like a knife cutting through butter. Soaring high, the view was breathtaking. I could see the different habitats, from woodland to marsh, to lake, to grassland. I landed for dinner as I had some juicy berries stored in my nest on the tallest tree.

It was afternoon, I had my feast and went flying. I was still hungry so I searched for some grain; I could see some plump grain down below. I swooped down as fast as I could so no other creature could eat it before me. Greedily, I grabbed the grain and I devoured it. The taste was sensational.

A flash of blue grey plummets past, it was a peregrine falcon. I took off as fast as a cheetah. I found sanctuary inside my home and waited for my predator to fly away. After waiting some time it gave up. I headed back out. It was safe, so I went to sleep, storing energy so that I could explore new ground as soon as I awoke.

Facts

Common name: Wood Pigeon
Scientific name: Columba Palumbus
Status: Least concern
Size: Wingspan 75-80cm. Length 40-42cm. Weight 450-550g.

Adaptations
The wood pigeon has a white, green, pink and purple neck, and a yellow, orange and red beak. It also has a grey and white body, with a white, black, grey and brown tail. It has scratching feet, which allow it to perch on branches and balance. Its beak is used to eat fruit, seeds and other plants. It takes off from its perch with a loud clattering. Flocks roost and feed together, but each bird maintains its own individual distance. Wood pigeons can live up to 16 years.

Habitat
You can see wood pigeons all year round and generally find them in gardens and woodland areas. Their habitat would be in a woodland area with shady trees such as those located in Potteric Carr, near Decoy Marsh, Willow Marsh and the Loversall filtration system.

Interdependence
The wood pigeon is a herbivore which means that it eats plants and grain, and not other animals. The start of its food chain is grain or plants, which is the producer. The wood pigeon is the secondary consumer, whilst the peregrine falcon is the apex predator. This means the wood pigeon needs to be aware, or it may get eaten.

Did you know?
It takes 14 days for their eggs to hatch and a further 30 to 34 days for the chick to fledge. It takes a young wood pigeon 16 weeks to get its distinctive white neck ring.

Blackbird (female)

I fly through the intense sky, overlooking a densely packed woodland with lots of different species. I flap my wings as fast as a cheetah rips its prey apart. I decided it was time for a meal so I landed and peaked at the dense soil and I find some worms. After a meal for one, I head home and settle in for bed because it's been a long day for me. As I fall asleep, I think to myself what tomorrow is going to be like for me, I might go on an adventure around Potteric Carr.

I awaken from a deep sleep in the beautiful woodland, where I spend most of my time looking at the crunchy brown leaves, the skeleton thin branches and the ivy like twigs. I enjoy the woodland, there is more to explore, more to see, more to scavenge.

I run off the tall, slim tree but as I do, I see a magnificent blackbird so I decide to show off my dazzling flying skills. I land next to him, my sharpened claws digging deep into the branch. We share each other's company for a little while, until he has to go. I tweet, 'see you around'.

I finally take my adventure to Potteric Carr, it is beautiful there with loads to explore like the woods and bird hides. I like it here, I might move in. The people who work here take great care of you and they provide you with a bird home and food like worms, slugs, windfall fruit, berries from shrubs, climbers and trees.

Facts

Common name: Blackbird (female)
Scientific name: Turdus merula
Status: Least concern
Size: Wingspan 35-38cm. Length 24-29cm. Weight 80-125g.

Adaptations
A male's colours are black feathers with a bright yellow beak and yellow ring around the eye. The female has brown feathers with a lighter breast and a brown beak. The blackbird has a slightly long beak so it can pick up its food easily. The common blackbird has feathers to insulate it from the sun and heat. They get their heat from flight. They also have amazing eyesight, so they can spot their next meal. They fly over fields to look for prey.

Habitat
You can find them in nature reserves like Potteric Carr, because there's lots of worms, slugs, windfall fruit, berries and trees. These birds love lawns and freshly-dug land, because that is where most of the worms are. Their habitat is woodland, but they adapt to other environments like farms, parks and gardens.

Interdependence
Grass (producer) > Worm (primary consumer) > Blackbird (secondary consumer) > Hawk (apex predator).
The blackbird is a secondary consumer, because it eats worms. It is prey to hawks, which are the apex predator at the top of the food chain.

Did you know?
Blackbirds are what is known as sexually dimorphic, which means that the plumage of the female is completely different to that of the male.

Coot

I stand as still as a rock, gazing across the damp wetland. Sunrise shines over the water. I hear the birds tweeting in the early morning; the noise rising above that of the gentle wind. I launch into the water, propelling myself along with my webbed feet. Calmly floating along the fresh cold water, a sudden burst of sunlight shines over the reflection of the trees.

Hopping out of the water, sticks snap and echo in my ears. I shake off the cold water, and rest on the damp grass. Whilst resting, I smell the fresh flowing water. The surface is disrupted by exploding water droplets. As I glide through the water, the waves push me like a boat in a storm.

I finally reach my destination, and suddenly everything is calm and quiet.

Facts

Common name: Coot
Scientific name: Fulica
Status: Least concern
Size: Wingspan 58–71cm. Length 34–43cm.

Adaptations
The coot has black feathers with a bright white beak and crown. It has big, lobed feet for wading in wetland. Its general colour is black and grey. Its short, wide wings are perfect for lifting off to fly. To start flying, it runs across the water using its feet and flaps its wings to create the uplift.

Habitat
You would be most likely to find the coot in a damp wetland and mostly in the lakes. This species is just a calm waterbird that enjoys the waters of habitats such as Potteric Carr. You can also find them on freshwater lakes, gravel pits, reservoirs, rivers and lakes, and they can sometimes be seen offshore.

Interdependence
In the food chain, the algae (producer) gets eaten by the tadpole (primary consumer) and they get eaten by the snail (secondary consumer). Then, the snail gets eaten by the coot.

Did you know?
The phrase 'bald as a coot' refers to white patch on the coot's head which looks a little like a bald spot.

Moorhen

I wake up and the sun is beating down on my black and white feathers. I swim out of my nest that I've crafted out of twigs, plants and reeds. The heat is getting unbearable. I start getting warm, so I waddle over to some shade.

I dive under the clear, freshwater to grab my breakfast of seeds. The seeds taste so lovely and amazing. I start swimming on the lake. I see another moorhen, so I swim over to it at the lake shore. I suddenly stop, because I see a big evil looking fox and I don't want to get hurt or killed.

Next, I pull some plants up near my nest to provide a protective cover from flooding, and to keep it from floating away. I swim around the lake for a little time then feel hungry, so I dive into the water and scoop up some unbelievable tasting leaves that are floating on the dismal dark water. The water is like stars shining on a lake on a twilight evening.

Facts

Common name: Moorhen
Scientific name: Gallinula chloropus
Status: Least concern
Size: Wingspan 50-55cm. Length 30-35cm. Weight 250-400g.

Adaptations
Moorhens are very sociable birds. They spend their lives in groups known as flocks. Moorhens have short wings, and as a result, are better swimmers and walkers, than flyers. When the moorhen swims, it bobs its head back and forth.

Habitat
You are most likely to find the moorhen on lakes, rivers, canals and ponds. They are black, with a red and yellow beak and long, green legs. They have a dark brown back and wings, and a more bluish-black belly. They also have vertical white stripes on their sides. Moorhens spend their life on the water. They have a number of adaptations including lobed toes, which aid the moorhen in both swimming and walking around the shallow banks of the water. At Potteric Carr, you will find the moorhen at Willow Marsh.

Interdependence
A moorhen's food chain begins with grass; the producer. The primary consumer is a worm. The primary consumer eats the producer. The secondary consumer is the moorhen. The secondary consumer eats the primary consumer. The apex predator, e.g. a fox, eats the secondary consumer.

Did you know?
Moorhens have short, rounded wings, meaning they are not very strong fliers, although they can fly for long distances. The common moorhen, in particular, migrates up to 2,000 km.

Bullfinch

I darted through the trees like a javelin piercing the air. I scanned the horizon seeing many different things. I saw small birds, green foliage, the pink sky and the yellow sun rise. A beautiful breeze made its way in between my rose-breasted feathers. I dropped for my prey, even though gravity was against me. Smoothly, I spread my wings like butter on bread and fixed my sights on an unsuspecting insect. Like lightning, I took out my prey. I munched greedily on my prey, as its sweet taste satisfied my appetite.

I flew back across the marsh skimming through trees and bushes, delighting in my freedom. Suddenly, I glimpsed a small orange speck as I glided into the woodland. I get closer and closer, the speck getting bigger and bigger. It's a fox. He spots me, but he's no threat. I am well beyond his reach.

Without a care, I decide to fly back to my flock as my silver jacket catches the sun.

Facts

Common name: Bullfinch
Scientific name: Pyrrhula
Status: Least concern
Size: Wingspan 12cm. Length 6-9cm.

Adaptations
Bullfinches can adapt to the temperature, because the colour of their feathers become lighter. The colour of their wings become darker and their bellies lighter in colder temperatures. Also, their beaks are adapted to be short and stubby to feed on buds. The male's tail brightens up when they meet a mate.

Habitat
Bullfinches are usually found in parkland and where there are clear fields. You will find bullfinches mostly around Willow Marsh. You will find that the bullfinch moves with its family.

Interdependence
The bullfinch flies straight into their prey, such as small insects. It doesn't have a lot of predators, but it is sometimes preyed upon by foxes, snakes and bigger birds.

Did you know?
Bullfinches can fly into water for small fish. It has a quiet call when it is in a small flock. Baby bullfinches are blind. The bullfinch can often damage fruit trees by feeding on developing buds.

Dunnock

It is deep into the afternoon. The surroundings are peaceful and picturesque. As I fly, I can feel the air's heavy atmosphere pushing me back. I am hitting an invisible barrier. My feathers are insulating me from the sun's heat. It's as if the air is on fire. I can see the trees deep down in the wood, screeching in horror, praying for mother nature to quench their thirst.

As I soar, I have a sense that my next meal is lurking in the field below. I cautiously fly in circles hovering nearer and nearer to the ground. My senses are correct, my meal is there. Three super-sized spiders scuttling and scattering. I swoop down sharply, and in a flash, they are gone. Not even a trace of blood.

Blissfully soaring over the water, I can see a colourful, scaley shimmer on the surface of the water. I fly lower for a closer look. I see a huge stickleback gliding, glimmering and glistening in the sunlit water. My claws scrape across the surface of the water, leaving a ripple and a tranquil image.

Afternoon turns to evening and evening turns to night. The nocturnals come out, and the rest of us go to our nests. I go to my small nest and the males are feeding my baby dunnocks; their last digestion for the day. I perch myself on a branch above with a perfect view of the calm water. As the sun disappears behind the hills in burning oranges, so do my cares and worries. I am taken into a relaxing trance.

Facts

Common name: Dunnock
Scientific name: Prunella modularis
Status: Moderate concern
Size: Wingspan 19-21cm. Length 13.5-14cm.

Adaptations
The dunnock is a small bird the size of a robin but the colours are light brown, red, grey and dark brown. They also have a sharp, thin bill to help it pick up insects such as beetles while feeding. They also are always really hot because of flight so they have feathers to insulate them from the sun and heat. Like all birds the dunnock has amazing eyesight to spot their next meal. You may see this being used when they are flying over fields.

Habitat
You are mostly likely to find dunnocks in places like hedgerows, gardens, or other places like nature reserves, which are attractive to a variety of other species. At Potteric Carr, you could find the dunnock at Corbett Wood, Seven Arches Carr and Loversall Carr. You could also try Willow Marsh.

Interdependence
A food chain represents what the animal eats and what eats the animal. The arrows show which way the energy travels. e.g. Nectar > Fly > Spider > Dunnock. Dunnocks feeds on insects and spiders, making it a secondary or tertiary consumer.

Did you know?
When dunnock chicks are born, they are fed by a few different male dunnocks instead of the mother. It is uncommon for a bird to have this behavior.

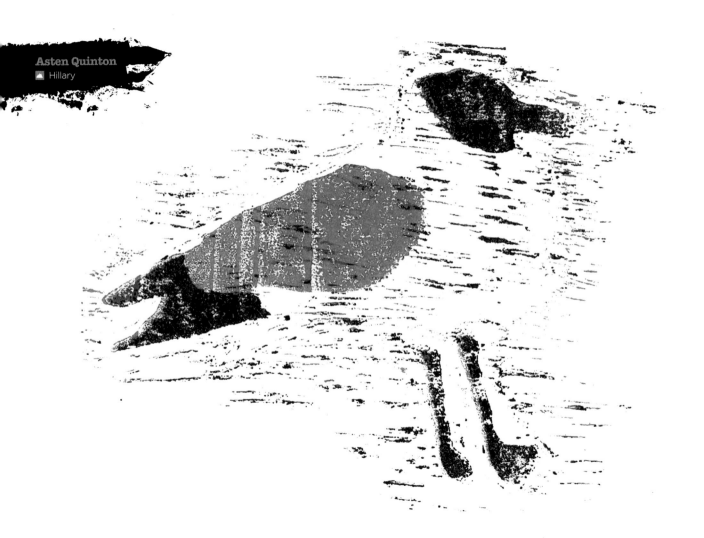

Black Headed Gull

When I am in my nest, the night comes quickly. As I am sleeping in my nest I have a wonderful dream, a dream about mating season. I am gliding as the wind pushes against my wings. My mate is waiting at home, with no danger to be found. My life then and now is wonderful. I have never complained, and I guarantee you I never will.

My mate and I noticed that we are different and the same when we looked our reflections in a puddle. Then, we saw four blobs in the sky. They were four beautiful American goldfinches – no danger to any of us.

As I awake from my slumber, the sun is just about to rise. Whenever a sunrise as beautiful as this happens, I keep thinking to myself, my children will return, my children will return. I race along the open water, not caring at all about stopping. As I kick my webbed feet through the clear water, a panic began. Anxiety began, and a lump rose in my throat. Where were they?

Then I saw a bittern having its first meal of the day, an eel, as I landed I silently sneaked up to the bittern, took its meal and flew off. As I hurried back to the nest, I heard a painful screech. I got back to the nest. It was too late. My partner was gone.

The next day I decided to stay in the nest. After all I have only got a few weeks to live, being almost at the end of my 32 years. My fulfilling life was happier when my mate was beside me.

Facts

Common name: Black Headed Gull
Scientific name: Chroicocephalus ridibundus
Status: Least concern
Size: Wingspan 100-110cm. Length 34-37cm. Weight 200-400g.

Adaptations
The black headed gull used to have a red tail, but then they adapted to migrating and now they have black and white tails. They've also adapted to swimming, so they now have webbed feet. The black headed gull, classed as a fierce predator, glides in a solid position as it hunts. Most of the time, they only ever migrate if there is no food left for them.

Habitat
You will find that black headed gulls live in marshy areas, but when mating season arrives they migrate to North-America to breed. When winter comes they migrate to coastal marshes, farmland, rubbish tips, urban parks, gardens and playing fields. They have unusual breeding habitats such as marshes, ponds, lakes, bogs, gravel pits and dry sites next to water bodies, such as sand-dunes and moorland.

Interdependence
The black headed gull will eat almost anything, including worms and small fish. It will also steal food from others. Luckily for the black headed gull, it is an apex predator, meaning it is at the top of the food chain with no natural predators. Because of this, their average lifespan is 32 years.

Did you know?
Black headed gulls can drink salt water as well as fresh water, as they possess special glands located in a part of the skull.

Kestrel

In the peaceful woodland, no prey to be seen, the sun rising and the whistling wind swaying the trees from side to side, makes me feel at home.

The night was cold but the day is warm. I set off, gliding through the soft, breezy air. The wind is passing through my silky soft, delicate wings, enveloping my tiny, fragile body. The wind lifts my body, making me feel as if someone has just walked over my awaiting grave. I become cold. Nothing around me; I am alone!

When I fly, I feel free, like nothing can stop me! I can fly above the treetops, swooping in, out, round and round. Nothing can stop me! My view is perfect. As I look down, I see greenery, moors and rivers. Being a kestrel, this most beautiful view is one of my most precious gifts.

I can hear my prey. A vole rustling in the brambles. Calling out to me, as if to say they want to be eaten. Waiting for me to pounce. I see my prey. I hover, waiting, scanning the ground for multiple amounts of voles. When they turn their backs, that's my cue to swoop in.

I dive straight down, piercing the air like a bullet. I am quickly nowhere to be seen, inside the brambles, latching my sharp claws onto the back of the vole. With a firm grip onto my victim, I take off with my prey to a nearby post.

Facts

Common name: Kestrel
Scientific name: Falco tinnunculus
Status: Moderate concern
Size: Wingspan 25-35cm. Length 25-35cm. Weight 140-200g.

Adaptations
You can spot a kestrel by looking for a hovering bird with a long tail and long wings that are blunt. When hovering, the tail goes into a fan shape. They are very easy to spot as they are one of the smaller birds of prey and because of its distinctive hover, scanning the ground below for prey. Kestrels can kill and carry more than one prey at a time, they will then sometimes take their prey to their nests to store it for later.

Habitat
You can often find kestrels in moors, heath, meadows and farmland. At Potteric you are likely to see a kestrel anywhere near hedgerows. Habitats not favoured by kestrels are dense woodlands, mountains and treeless wetlands. This is because dense forests and woodland have too many trees whereas treeless land and mountains don't tend to have anywhere for them to perch. You can see kestrels all year round.

Interdependence
A kestrel is a carnivore. It eats primary consumers and secondary consumers such as mice, voles, worms and other small mammals. The kestrel does not have any predators and so it is an apex predators. Kestrels have to eat 4-8 voles a day to survive.

Did you know?
Kestrels are fully protected under the Wildlife and Countryside Act, since 1981. This makes it a bad idea to kill, take or injure a kestrel!

Great Tit

As I lie there, motionless, the crunch of dry autumn leaves and the sweet birdsong of the coal tit seems to be the only sound for miles, surrounding me like a harmonic cocoon, gently lulling me into my dreams. I drift slowly away, as I nestle into my soft fluffy wings. The moon glimmers across the marshland and my eyes droop to a close.

I awaken, the crisp morning air brushing through my feathers as my eyes widen and I become alert once more. The wind brushes against the water's edge, rippling its silky smooth surface as the sun's reflection becomes a blur within an ocean of blue. Then a grumble, followed by a sharp stabbing pain. Hunger ensues. I need to find food and fast.

I take to the skies as my feathers ripple against the howling wind. I join another juvenile, a blue tit, before parting once more. I settle on a branch, then a flash of emerald amongst the dense woodland. My prey awaits. I dip down, brushing the neon grass as I clench the small winged creature with my short curved beak, slowly crushing it's crunchy crisp shell as it falls into a state of paralysis. I pin it down with my sharp curved claw as I slowly tear away at its bright green flesh. No grasshopper stands a chance.

My stomach smiles as my hunger suppresses, and I return to my usual state of being. Calm and soothed, I return to my nest to prepare for my afternoon hunt.

Facts

Common name: Great Tit
Scientific name: Parus major
Status: Least concern
Size: Wingspan 22-25cm. Length 14cm. Weight 16-21g.

Adaptations
The great tit has many adaptations to make it best suited to its environment. One physiological adaptation is a thin layer of fur beneath the feathers to insulate it and keep it warm. The great tit has a small curved beak to reach for grubs in tight places and small sharp talons to provide grip. Great tits like to nest in trees to provide shelter and protection from predators, as well as nesting near grassy patches due to their high grasshopper population.

Habitat
You can find great tits in parks, forests and gardens across most of the UK nesting in leafy shaded trees, high up in the branches away from predators. Great tits can be found at Potteric Carr, in Willow and Piper Marshes due to the amount of trees and food sources nearby.

Interdependence
A common food chain of the great tit shows them as a secondary consumer with their common prey being grasshoppers (consumer) whose primary food is grass (producer). Great tits can fall prey to hunting birds such as sparrowhawks.

Did you know?
Great tits have one of the strongest beaks of the tit family. It is so strong, it can crack hazel and beech nuts with no help!

Chaffinch

Thunder, roaring like a lion, wakes me. I jump to my feet, my claws clutched to the bottom of the nest, my heart beating faster than speed itself. My body stiff as a surfboard, frightened by the pelting rain, shaking my nest.

The tree where my nest is shakes violently, twigs catapulting around my nest. Am I in the midst of a nightmare? I am despondent. Then, suddenly, before my eyes it dawns on me, I have to escape. Hurling my shaking body into the terrifying air, I am tossed around like a ragdoll in this angry whirlwind.

The explosive wind, sounding like a thousand lost souls, overpowers my ears. I feel helpless. Subdued by mother nature. Dramatically, I am thrown against a tree then, like a rock, I fall to the ground. I can't stand. To my horror, I can't fly. My wing is broken, the pain is unbearable. Is this the end?

Facts

Common name: Chaffinch
Scientific name: Fringilla coelebs
Status: Very common
Size: Wingspan 24.5-28.5cm. Length 14.5cm.

Adaptations
A chaffinch has a beak designed for cracking nuts. The male is burgundy, blue, white and black. Females are brown, black and white.

Habitat
You can see the chaffinch around the UK in woodland, fields, parks and gardens. Chaffinches are found all over the world from New Zealand to the UK. You can find the Chaffinch in wooded areas around Potteric Carr, such as the paths around Willow Marsh.

Interdependence
The chaffinch mostly eats seeds, but when they are young, the mothers feed them insects. Adults mostly eat insects in breeding season. Chaffinches are commonly hunted by predators such as the sparrow hawk.

Did you know?
Chaffinches often have accents which vary depending on the part of the country they live in.

Kingfisher

The wind pushes against my glistening blue and orange feathers, the skeleton brown branches of trees dancing with the wind blurred in my peripheral vision. I hear birds singing morning carols of joy, and the hubbub of geese awakening from a deep slumber. I look down and as if in slow motion, I see shimmering water and multiple insects gliding along the surface, the distinctive smell of a spring morning and fresh dew drops rising through my streamlined nostrils. The warm morning sun drumming down on my brightly coloured feathers.

I suddenly see a small movement in the still water below, a slight ripple occurs. I beat my wings, rising through the sky, my head focused. My eyes lock onto a target, I gain a slight bit of speed and then initiate my dive, like a torpedo my long body moves at an extreme speed. Without a drop of water rising I pierce the water like an olympic diver, my beak pointed and aiming for my prey. I stab the small fish like a medieval fighter and then rise upwards, my trajectory, the tree branch. I perch on the branch shaking the water off like a dog that had just finished swimming. I drop the fish onto the hazel branches and peck at it, I then gulp down the fish's slippery body.

My bright feathers glistening after the quick wash, they can tell I'm an apex predator. I observe my surroundings gazing at the still water and glancing at the waving trees. Waiting for the perfect time to start another razor sharp attack.

Facts

Common name: Kingfisher
Scientific name: Alcedines
Status: Moderate concern
Size: Wingspan 25cm. Length 16cm. Weight 34-46g.

Adaptations
Kingfishers have a long pointed beak that is extremely aerodynamic and can pierce the water effectively, which helps with hunting accuracy and damage to prey. It also has short specially shaped wings that can be tucked into its body at a moment's notice, and as a result the diving speed sharply increases. They can be identified by their beautiful shimmering coat of bright blue and a majestic orange. A beneficial behavioural adaptation is that they like to stay around their hunting grounds, meaning less effort is needed to catch its next meal.

Habitat
In the warmer months of the year, you can find kingfishers playfully jumping from branch to branch or flying at incredible speeds, so you'll need to be quick if you want to catch a glimpse. They specifically prefer to be near still or slow flowing water, such as Willow Marsh, where they will catch the majority of their food.

Interdependence
The kingfisher depends on small fish and small insects and is perfectly adapted to catch these. Unfortunately this is not an apex predator so it does have natural predators e.g: foxes, large birds and cats. However most of these predators have to surprise the kingfisher as it is too quick for most of them.

Did you know?
The kingfisher is a very quick bird (20mph) that is so small and agile it can sometimes fly past predators undetected.

Mallard

The sun rises and the red sky is beautiful. I can feel the calm water around me. It is amazingly relaxing. The reflection of the sun glitters in my eye, whilst it beams down until it hits my back. Using my beady eyes to look for those juicy water elm which I eat for breakfast, I dip my head into the wavy water. I lift my head out of the lake with a bundle of water elm stuffed in my mouth. My emerald green feathers glisten in the morning sunlight, as droplets of water drip off my head. I get the taste of the delicious plant as I take a bite of my feast. The taste of the water elm rushes through my body.

I haven't been here long as I've just migrated from the Lakeside. The current of the lake drifts around me. As I elegantly glide on the surface of the water, there are many other birds here, nearly all of which are swimming gently. Unfortunately, rain appears and all the other birds look for shelter. The rain has never bothered me.

I find myself on a mini island, so I decide to perch on it. I get comfortable and fall to sleep quicker than the speed of light, due to a busy day's exploring.

Facts

Common name: Mallard
Scientific name: Anas platyrhynchos
Status: Least concern
Size: Wingspan 81-98cm. Length 50-62cm. Weight 850-1500g.

Adaptations
These birds have developed features that enable them to blend into their habitat quite well. It may be difficult to see the female mallards if they are in reedbeds as they have camouflaged feathers. Males are easily identified by their beautiful, dark green heads and bright yellow bills. They wear a warm layer of down feathers that are waterproof. They have powerful muscles in their chest to give them the strength to fly long distances, webbed feet for swimming, and a flat curved bill for eating different types of food. They normally nest close to water.

Habitat
You can find mallards in a lake, pond or a river. They paddle on water like a pedal boat. At Willow Marsh this species is very common. The reason they like this area so much is because mallards live in a marshy area. To see this bird you don't have to look very hard as they are quite common and aren't very shy.

Interdependence
The mallard is a primary consumer and will eat things like water elm seeds. Unfortunately for the mallard it has predators this means it may get eaten. In a food chain the mallard would be a secondary consumer.

Did you know?
Mallards are thought to be the most abundant duck on Earth.

Bittern

My head suddenly drops into the water before emerging again a second later with a writhing fish gripped in my beak. Eating my final meal of the day, I begin to stalk back across the mudflats. The sun reluctantly starts to drop below the horizon and the wind whistles through a nearby reedbed; the same wind that is blowing past my face and ruffling my feathers. All around me echoes the deep, booming mating calls of other males competing for the last female bitterns. I have no need for such a practice as I have already mated and have four eggs hidden away among the reeds.

Weaving through the spindly, golden towers that are my home, I suddenly freeze. Directly ahead of me, at the border of the woodland, a fox is perched atop a mound of earth; alert, vigilant, listening, like a sentry. My instincts suddenly spring to life. I outstretch my neck, beak pointed at the sky, perfectly still. A slight breeze picks up, so I sway with it, just like the countless reeds surrounding me. Then, as suddenly as he appeared, the fox bounds off into the trees, presumably in pursuit of a hare or rabbit. With the danger gone, I resume my journey.

I arrive back at my nest, and thankfully find it intact, a perfectly shaped platform of reeds, containing four small, white eggs. Watching over and incubating these eggs is another bittern: their mother. With the sun having completely vanished now, its presence known only by the orange stain it has left on the horizon, I curl up for the night, hidden among the reeds.

Facts

Common name: Bittern
Scientific name: Botaurus stellaris
Status: High concern
Size: Wingspan 100-130cm. Length 69-81cm. Weight 870-1940g.

Adaptations
The bittern is perfectly adapted to its environment. Its anatomical adaptations include its feathers, which perfectly camouflage it among the reeds. The bittern has long legs with large feet to help it to move through reedbeds. One of its most outstanding behavioural adaptations is the 'booming' call that males make when looking to attract a mate, beginning in late January.

Habitat
You can find the bittern in mudflats with large reed beds, such as Decoy Marsh at Potteric Carr, where they nest and hunt. You'll need to keep your eyes peeled as not only are they very rare, but they are also very well camouflaged. The bittern likes to nest among reeds, building a platform-like nest where females will lay 5-6 eggs which are then incubated.

Interdependence
The bittern eats a variety of items, including small fish, amphibians and eels. However, the bittern is an apex predator and has no natural predators. Despite this, a bittern will normally only live for around 8 years.

Did you know?
One of the bittern's many nicknames is 'butter bump', referring to its high fat content.

Greylag Goose

I sit on an island and survey my surroundings. I watch the Canada geese families around me, the hatchlings and goslings chirping in my ear, enjoying the delightful taste of worms and grubs.

I felt like taking a leisurely swim in the murky water. The smooth swaying movement of the water underneath me massaged my feet softly, my feet immersed. I felt my webbed feet no more. They were numb.

Short broken trees fall down from the strong wind. I look out for the kestrels that I fear want to tear me to shreds. They're like predatory leopards waiting to pounce on their prey. The soothing summer breeze moves me from side to side. My fellow Canada geese fly above me, covering me in shadows.

I glance up to see the immense, grey barriers in the sky, hiding the sun as it turns to a dull day. The barriers are grey then white, then finally blue as I fly up above. It suddenly turns cold, so I waddle back onto the island close to me, surrounded by the seagulls and geese, hatchlings and goslings.

I am hungry. I need food. I walk to find a perfect patch of fresh green grass to eat. I find it. I can't bear the pain any more. I dive in straight away.

As the day comes to an end, I finish my journey outside of the lake, and begin my long and heavy voyage back to my homeland.

Facts

Common name: Greylag Goose
Scientific name: Anser anser
Status: Least concern
Size: Wingspan 149-168cm. Length 74-84cm.

Adaptations
You can identify greylag geese easily because of their bright orange bill, pink legs and black tail. Most of their body is grey, with a pale feather edging and a white rump. Greylag geese stay together in a herd for a long time and are usually found flying in large flocks. In breeding season, between September and January, you can find greylag geese feeding in groups.

Habitat
You can find greylag geese in different habitats such as lakes and grown fields. The place that you are most likely to find greylag geese in Potteric Carr is at Decoy Lake, which is marshy land with a reedbed.

Interdependence
The greylag goose is a herbivore and a primary consumer, mainly eating grass and reeds. It is preyed upon by kestrels, which are apex predators.

Did you know?
Greylag geese are found all over the world and show slight variations in colour. The Siberian birds have slightly lighter heads and have lighter backs.

Cinnabar Moth

I dart away as fast as lightning as it starts to pour down with bombarding rain. I arrive at my warm, dry shelter. Everywhere I look, I can see nothing but colourful, common ragwort flowers, their heads ready to be devoured. I approach a tall, juicy flower and check to see that there's nothing already inside. It's empty, so I use my antenna to feed from it. The sweet nectar gives me the boost of energy that I need before I fall fast asleep.

I rest at the end of the day, after another journey out in the wilderness. As I quickly fly through the strong and powerful wind, it's a hard fight. It's near impossible to stay up in the air. I carefully weave through the sharp thorny bushes that are like blades. I fly over to rest in marshlands upon the reeds. As I dash from location to location, around the woodland, I realise I have no obvious home. I take comfort as the sun glimmers on my bright red wings, making them shine like a diamond.

Facts

Common name: Cinnabar Moth
Scientific name: Tyria jacobaeae
Status: Least concern
Size: Wingspan 32-43mm. Length 20mm. Weight 560g.

Adaptations
If you are out around the reserve at Potteric Carr, and you notice what you think is a butterfly, with bright red markings on the forewing and the hind wings mostly red, it is probably the cinnabar moth. This a medium-sized black moth. It flies in the day and sleeps at night (diurnal).

Habitat
The time of year that you are most likely to see a cinnabar moth is around May. You are likely to find it in places such as waste grounds, railway banks, woodland and grassland.

Interdependence
The cinnabar moth is a primary consumer. When they are caterpillars, they eat poisonous ragwort. Adults feed off the leaves and flowers of the common ragwort, and are occasionally found on other ragworts and groundsels.
The predators of a cinnabar moth are birds, such as cuckoos.

Did you know?
In parts of the world, the cinnabar moth is used to control the invasive and poisonous plant, tansy ragwort. A female can lay up to 300 eggs in their lifetime, with normally around 30-40 laid at a time.

Great Crested Newt

As I rise from my soothing slumber, I hear the wind gently breathing out a cold breeze. I hear the blackbirds, pigeons and other birds constructing an orchestra of calls that are a mixture of distress, happiness and defence, the sound of which thickens the cold air. I decide to wander out of my rocky outcrop into the wetland and plunge into the transparent water. I feel resistance as I pierce through the turbulent surface like a bullet piercing through a body.

Basking in the calm water, waiting to strike, I catch a sudden movement. Stealthily, I transform my posture from the shape of a small stone into a leopard hunting its prey with high precision. The wind becomes stronger and with every blow it spits out raging gusts of rain. The water rages again, angered, changing from a calm tremor in the water to a tsunami. Within this whirlwind, I catch the dazzling dragonfly larvae. I crush it with my piston jaws and consume it with one gulp, swallowing it down into the acidic liquids lingering inside my body. Then I stop.

I sight the lumbering giant that is a heron. Stopping in my tracks, I covertly sink my feet into the mud as I wait for the predator to go. After it lumbers away, I dart through the onslaught of water into a moss infested ledge and climb back up. Then I scan the area and wander back to the rocky outcrop and lie under a stone. I observe the glistening giant in the sky as it retreats as the stars awake and brighten the darkening night sky.

Facts

Common name: Great Crested Newt
Scientific name: Triturus cristatus
Status: Least concern
Size: Length 15-17cm. Weight 10g.

Adaptations
You can identify a great crested newt because of the small paper white spots that cover the body on both sides. To identify a male great crested newt, look for the spikes on its back. You might notice it has webbed feet, enabling it to swim fast in the water. As it swims, it can extract oxygen from the water through its skin. They sometimes wander over 1km to find a mating partner, and lay eggs that are submerged in water. Like all amphibians, their eggs are soft rather than hard, like with the eggs of reptiles such as lizards.

Habitat
You can often find great crested newts in hedges and ditches. They can be found in most parts of Potteric Carr, including Willow Marsh. The best time to see them would be the summer months of July and August.

Interdependence
The great crested newts predators are badgers, heron and foxes. It is a tertiary consumer which means it consumes other predators and so is a carnivore. The great crested newt eats dragon fly larvae, dragonflies and other aquatic insects which are secondary consumers.

Did you know?
The great crested newt can regenerate limbs such as legs, tails and even the lenses in the centre of their eyes.

Azriel Chan
⚡ Franklin

Common Darter

A light cool breeze shook the trees in the sunny wetland as I stood astutely upon a thick, leafy branch. Looking out across the seemingly endless fields, I realised that the sun had flown further into the blue oblivion. Whilst it continued to warm my skin, I readied myself for flight: I crawled forward to the edge of the branch; faster and faster, my wings mobilized. Once my wings were moving at full speed, I tucked my legs in. Not waiting another moment, I took off.

Propelling myself swiftly across the large meadows, I heard the continuous buzzing of my wings as I soared through the pleasant air. I headed past a small, deep marsh and into the grand forest. As I continued to delve into the reserve, I began to fight the wild winds. Suddenly, I stopped; a lone mosquito had caught my eye.

Taking the mosquito's position and movement into consideration, I landed on a branch overhanging the insect's route. As it flew past beneath me, I realised it was my time to strike. I left the branch, chasing the mosquito through the bracken entangled maze as fast as I could. I trailed the mosquito deeper into the forest, narrowly escaping the clutches of the many alders and silver birches that engulfed the creatures living on the soft, soil floor.

Faster and faster, I closed in on my objective. Quickly, with ease, I clenched it between my thirsty jaws. From here, I brought it to a nearby branch where I held it in a steady position so that I could satisfy my hunger. Very proud with my latest kill, I reflected on the rest of the day.

Facts

Common name: Common Darter
Scientific name: Sympetrum striolatum
Status: Least concern
Size: Length 38-43mm. Wingspan 58mm approx.

Adaptations
You can spot a common darter by looking out for their long red tail, blurry wings and large, ball-shaped eyes. Common darters have special chemicals in their stomach that allow them to digest any prey they capture, allowing them to eat a wider range of food. If you look carefully, you may see a common darter perched high waiting to ambush its prey. Common darters are territorial over breeding waters and chase other insects away. They dart around quickly, hovering from place to place.

Habitat
You will be able to find common darters frequently around ponds and lakes. However, they also can be found resting on the tops of plants in woodland areas. If you visit Potteric Carr, you may be able to find them in Loversall Field. Mainly a summer and autumn species, they can be found well into November.

Interdependence
The common darter is a carnivore, and a secondary consumer. They eat just about any prey they can catch: mainly flying insects such as midges, flies or mosquitoes. They do not have any predators because they are so fast. However, as they age, they may be picked off by frogs or predatory birds.

Did you know?
Usually, common darters live for 1-2 weeks, but in some rare cases they live up to 6-8 weeks old!

Water Spider

My habitat is a dense, dirty, green wetland.

As I sit here like a statue, the rain droplets hit me like a herd of charging rhinos. Whilst I'm sitting here, still and silent, I can identify the rain droplets hitting the gentle water and making ripples. Even though the rain is as loud as sirens, I can still hear other species chirping, croaking, tweeting happily away.

As I begin to hunt, I'm as poised as a panther, while I watch and observe my prey. All of a sudden, I pounce on my prey. A scaly, white, freshwater shrimp, in the transparent water. Once I have my prey under control, I violently inject my venom into the helpless shrimp's body. Once my venom's inside my prey, I devour it all. Once I had swallowed my kill, the only taste in my mouth was the succulent meat of the recently-expired, freshwater shrimp.

Whilst I'm lying here relaxing on the bottom of the deserted river bed, after my feast, I can see my prey and my predators clearly from all angles.

Facts

Common name: Water Spider
Scientific name: Argyroneta aquatica
Status: Least concern
Size: Male leg span 7.8-18.7mm. Female leg span 7.8-13.1mm.

Adaptations
You will find it hard to see the water spider because it has adapted to live underwater and rarely comes up to the surface. Water spiders also can maintain cocoons (water bubbles) underwater so they can breath and only need to come up to the surface once a day. They live their entire lives underwater where they mate, lay eggs and catch prey.

Habitat
You can often find the water spider in wetlands, lakes, ponds and streams. These habitats are often in northern and central Europe. To find the water spider around Potteric Carr, go to Reedbed Filtration System, Decoy Marsh, Willow Marsh or Beeston Plantation.

Interdependence
The predators of the water spider are the pike, frogs and kestrels. Also, their prey are aquatic animals like freshwater shrimps, water beetles and the whirligig beetle. The water spider is an omnivore. It mainly eats primary consumers, so the water spider is a secondary consumer.

Did you know?
Did you know that this is one of few spider species where the male is larger than the female.

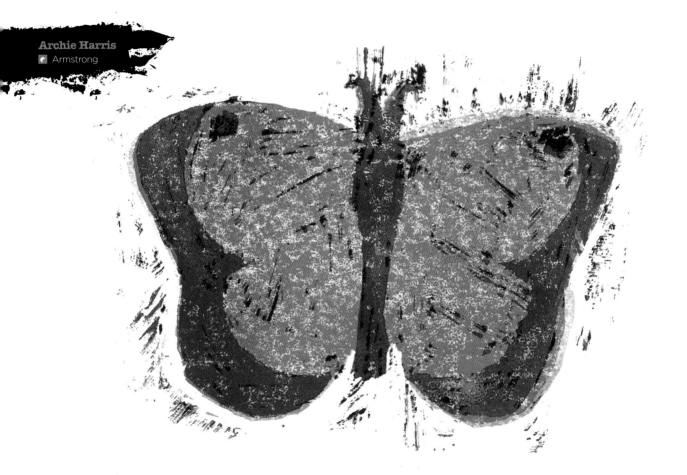

Gatekeeper Butterfly

I flew across the meadow, taking in all the scents of the flowers. The grass brushing against my stomach, the wind brushing against my wings, making me shiver with every gust. I landed on a plant and opened my wings and, all of a sudden, the wind swooped me up and into the sky. I glided as far as the wind took me, then I slowly landed next to a pond. Scarily, I was seconds away from being eaten by a frog, but I just got away and, with a lot of weariness on my side, I travelled home for a long rest.

I started again, flying over the flowers. They were like a giant sheet covering the earth as far as I could see. The smell filled my nose to the brim. I flew so low that I could feel the plants brushing against my abdomen. As I was enjoying myself, a finch glided out over me trying to catch me, but he got stuck in some thorns. I was safe once more.

Facts

Common name: Gatekeeper Butterfly
Scientific name: Pyronia tithonus
Status: Least concern
Size: Male length 37-43mm. Female length 42-48mm.

Adaptations
You can spot the gatekeeper butterfly with its orange and brown colour with black eye spots on the fore wing tip. They also have two white spots, not one as in the meadow brown butterfly. It stays on a flower for a long period of time to collect all the nectar. The gatekeeper changes from a caterpillar to a butterfly. This is called metamorphism.

Habitat
It lives in bushes and shrubbery where there is lots of food. At Potteric Carr, you are likely to encounter them in such habitats as Loversall field. It is also found near tall grass, or near heath and and down land. It may also be found in patches of shrubs under cliffs too.

Interdependence
It is a primary consumer and feeds on producers. This means it is a herbivore, because it only eats plants. It mainly eats foods such as brambles.

Did you know?
It is named the gatekeeper butterfly because it mainly lives in hedges near field gates. As a result, it is also nicknamed 'Hedge Brown'.

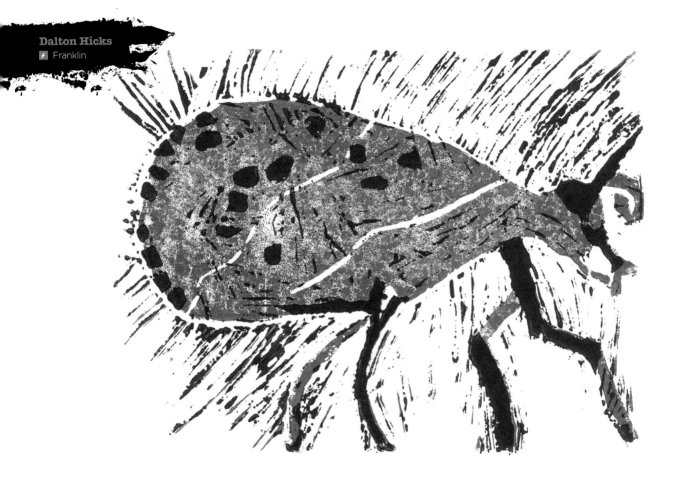

Caddisfly

I wake to the noise of the deadly, vibrant, burnt orange coy fish prowling down the shallow river searching for food. I quickly dip down into the river to my hiding spot, when the predator looks up at my sunset orange reed bed. Fortunately, my predator doesn't see me. He moves on slowly, so I shoot up to the top of the river like a firework. The sun beams down onto the river and reflects off into my reed bed. I look up at the azure bright sky, with white fluffy clouds like marshmallows towering over me.

I eat my liquid food, like a fish drinking the ocean. The reeds are high, the heavy rain is pouring down and pounding my skin like stones hitting a window. I see some more reed beds that I've never seen before, and they draw me in like a baby to a dummy. I open up my dull black and white camouflaged wings and I am on my way.

I finally get there. I soon come to realise why no creature goes there; it is surrounded by fish! I hide in the reed bed; I blend in like a ghillie suit. No fish sees me, but I can't fight because I am too flaccid and they can swallow me whole. I fly with the wind rushing past me, low, skimming the grass back to my reed bed. The fish is gone. I rest in my cozy reed bed. As the light sun falls and the pale moon rises, I sleep.

Facts

Common name: Caddisfly
Scientific name: Trichoptera
Status: Concerned
Size: Body length 20-40mm. Weight 76-124mg.

Adaptations
You might have trouble finding caddisflies because they are very small. You can identify a caddisfly by looking for something that looks like a fly near a freshwater habitat. If it is a caddisfly you might see it dip down into the water. Female caddisflies dip under water to lay their eggs. They are bugs, but they are also architects. They spin out silk which forms a casing to protect and camouflage them during metamorphosis. They do not develop mouthparts e.g. teeth, to break down the food, so can only feed on liquids.

Habitat
They construct protective shelters and are aquatic larvae. They like freshwater habitats and have specialised houses. As adults, like moths, they are attracted to light at night. You might find the caddisfly in freshwater habitats such as streams, lakes, rivers and ponds. In Potteric Carr, they can be found by the main ditch near the visitor entrance.

Interdependence
The caddisfly has few predators, however fish will eat them. They are not predators, because all they eat are producers, such as plant fluids and algae.

Did you know?
Caddisflies can only fly when adults, and live for just a few weeks. As adults, they do not feed at all.

Water Stick Insect

Sticking to my water-soaked leaf, I slowly proceed to drift across the motionless water, into the reedbeds. The reedbeds match my colour, shielding me, giving me a chance of survival against any dangerous and cruel predators. Mindful of this, I watch my immediate surroundings, scanning for the spiders and birds that could erase me from this wonderful world.

A spider spots me and is makes his way, closer and closer. As it swims up to the surface of the water, I make my plan to hide from it. Suddenly, a ravenous mouse swiftly moves up to it and eats the spider in one. Now that the gory scene ends, the mouse scurries away into the bushes. Relief.

Floating elegantly on the water, like a ballerina in a classical dance, slowly drifting towards the marshes, my eyes catch sight of some pickerelweed. I am delighted to see this sight, this will be my meal for the day. Hopping on to this delicious plant, I begin to nibble away to my heart's content. In the distance, I hear the piercing croak of a toad. I finish my delicious meal quickly, so the toad doesn't make a meal of me!

Facts

Common name: Water Stick Insect
Scientific name: Ranatra linearis
Status: Least concern
Size: Length 1.16cm-32.8cm or, over 55cm.

Adaptations
You can see anatomical adaptations of the water stick insect by looking at the long, thin brown body with a long tail. It also has long hooked front legs. The water stick insect has a long breathing tube which it uses as a snorkel when hunting its prey.

Habitat
You can locate the water stick insect in marshlands and reed beds. At Potteric Carr, you might find them in certain places such as the reedbed filtration system, Decoy Marsh or Low Ellers Marsh. Maybe you could try Beston Hide.

Interdependence
The water stick insect is a well adapted predator and will hunt other creatures such as tadpoles and small fish making it a secondary consumer.

Did you know?
The water stick insect has excellent camouflage and when it doesn't want to be seen, it can lay flat so that it looks just like a stick!

Straw Dot Moth

As my rapid wings beat through the rustling twigs, branches and leaves of the oak and birch trees, I fly like a surfer on a giant wave. As the heaving rain tries to pull me down, I dodge the explosive droplets. I knew if a single drop of the molten ice hit me, I'd be spiraling down like a helicopter in distress.

I scout for a delicious delicacy. I search the wet meadows and towering woods for an autumn gentia's nectar. I had craved this luscious nectar ever since I became a moth. I suddenly spotted its star-shaped petals, so I swooped and glided down to the glowing autumn gentia and drank its nectar.

After I had enjoyed this sumptuous drink, I hid away from my tweeting predators in a barbed den of thorns and brambles. The ongoing tweeting came closer... and closer... then the tweeting came to a sudden stop; the bird brushed past me without a single, soundless stare.

Facts

Common name: Straw Dot Moth
Scientific name: Rivula sericealis
Status: Least concern
Size: Wingspan 18-22mm

Adaptations
You can recognize a straw dot moth by the two dark brown/ black dots on its wings. You may see that a straw dot's wings and body are a lighter shade of brown and white. You might find it difficult to spot them because they have camouflage which blends in with the trees and they will fly and hide from their predator. The straw dot starts its life as an egg, then over time it changes form to a larva then again to a pupa and finally into an adult moth.

Habitat
You can find straw dot moths in moorland and woodland from June to September.

Interdependence
Straw dot moths are herbivores as well as a primary consumers. As adults, they eat nectar from flowers such as autumn gentian. As larvae, they eat grass, mainly purple moor grass and false brome grass. Straw dot moths are eaten by predators such as bats.

Did you know?
Straw dot moth larvae (caterpillars) are small. They are less than 2.5cm in length.

Froghopper

The morning sunlight blinds me as I jump from plant to plant for my morning feed. I land on a beautiful, green silk-thin, boat-like leaf. As I munch through the juicy but crunchy leaf, I suck the luscious sap out. Whilst I do this, I spot a terrifying spider, creeping closer, closer and closer, until suddenly, it attacks me. I escape from the predator by disappearing into my cocoon-type shell, made from the leaf sap. After a while, I wriggle out silently to see if the predator is gone. He's disappeared. Whilst crawling out of my protective shell, I find myself buried under a pile of heavy, large leaves. I tried to get up, but they were close to crushing me as I'm very small.

As I get on my way, climbing and scrambling through the terrific maze of crushing leaves, trying to catch my breath in the doomy maze. When, eventually, I get out and inhale, I jump as far away as possible, so I don't get crushed again. Whilst I bounce away, I find a perfect spot to have a nibble, keeping my nymphs and myself full. As I lay down, I spawn my eggs all over the leaves, I have around ten. They are in a protective cocoon of their own. I have done my job, I have played my part.

Facts

Common name: Froghopper
Scientific name: Cercopoidea
Status: Least concern
Size: Adults are oval, and 6-10mm in length.

Adaptations
You can identify adults with their dark brown body and two red/orange stripes. Nymphs are yellow to yellow/green, which helps them to camouflage. It spits frothy sap taken from plants to hide and protect itself from predators. You will need to look on leaves for the nymphs, which you will find inside white sap bubbles, commonly called cuckoo spit.

Habitat
You can often find froghoppers in grassland, heathland and woodland.

Interdependence
The froghopper is a herbivore and a primary consumer. They eat plant sap and, for example, nettle sap. Predators of a froghopper are birds, frogs, toads and spiders.

Did you know?
The froghopper recycles sap from grass stems by converting it to a soapy liquid, and then pumping it into foamy bubbles inside their tails.

Hawthorn Shield Bug

My habitat is the hawthorn bushes. The leaves are spiky sharp to others, but they are not to me. Surrounded by trees, it is quite shady here. Long grass waves at me in the breeze. I am settled in an extensive wood, not far from a small town. I hear other bugs and animals close to me, I can also hear the distant rumbling of vehicles. I hear the trains trundle clumsily along the tracks not far from me. Camouflaged, I blend into my sharp round leaf, so that I cannot be seen. The sky darkens to grey. I begin to panic as gigantic explosive droplets fall from above. I ineffectively attempt to dodge them but suddenly, I am hit.

I fall down and hit the wet mud with a thud. From where I stand I see a snail. It is enormous compared to me. The snail crawls incredibly slowly across the muddy floor. I creep past it and carry on my journey to find cover and return to my leaf. I slowly crawl across the open woodland where I am covered by a dark shadow. I look up to find that a blackbird is flying above me. It seems to have spotted me upon the rotting leaves. It swoops down and lands in front of me.

It places its beak in front of me and opens it up. It shoves its beak forward and I am now inside the blackbird's beak. I release my deadly weapon. A horrible stink that makes the bird spit me out instantly. It flies off into the distance. I am safe and feel a great sense of relief.

Facts

Common name: Hawthorn Shield Bug
Scientific name: Acanthosoma haemorrhoidale
Status: Least concern
Size: Length 13-15mm

Adaptations
The hawthorn shield bug feeds through the rostrum, a beak-like projection, which sucks liquidised plant tissue. It is semi-digested by the delivery of saliva. The anatomical adaptations are that it is camouflaged in shades of green and brown. Their compound eyes are coloured red. It's has six long, green stick-like legs. The hawthorn shield bug is attracted to lights at night.

Habitat
You are likely to find the hawthorn shield bug in hawthorn bushes and trees. You can also find this bug in places such as wood, heath and grasslands, small ponds or rivers, farms, towns and houses. At Potteric Carr, you'll find them in hawthorn trees and woodland. They eat haws, which are the fruit of hawthorn trees. Over the summer, the nymphs feed on ripening red berries. The time of the year you would find adult hawthorn shield bugs is around late August to late autumn. The eggs are laid in spring.

Interdependence
The hawthorn shield bug is a primary consumer and eats haws which grow on hawthorn trees and bushes. The hawthorn shield bug is occasionally eaten by blackbirds, which are secondary consumers. Blackbirds are eaten by sparrowhawks.

Did you know?
The hawthorn shield bug is known as the 'stink bug' as they release a powerful stench when disturbed.

Common Roach

The depth beneath me felt new, felt fresh. It's spring now. The gargantuan green leaves swooped down and landed peacefully on the face of the water, carried by the gradual current. As my eyes surveyed this blue vision, the trees' reflection emerged onto the crystal-like water. The surface of the water altered its mass, and made several shapes which gleamed in the afternoon sunlight. I scrunched up in an almost ball; a tribe of grey miniature figures rapidly collided with my delicate scales. Ignoring them, I surged and plunged through a dark, mysterious habitat. From the moment I encountered the pitch black expanse, the many species transpired. As I transferred myself, the reeds swayed and the water smiled maliciously as its toxic smell lingered in the air. Instantaneously, cascades of rain torrents arrived once more, but this time more substantially. Quickly I vanished, leaving the rain to barricade the smooth paper shredding on the rocks.

I gathered several reeds with my fins and concealed my body from the dead of the evening. Camouflaged, I hid within the deformed stone pebbles beneath my endangered habitat. Eventually, a figure-like shadow arrived above me. As quick as a lightning bolt, a beak dipped beneath the skyline of water and left volumes of water which covered the shelter. The treacherous creature caught its breath. Then, silence. Silence. Splash! Fortunately for me, the predator was unsuccessful. He flew off, leaving me with an overwhelming sense of relief. Eventually, I lifted my head above the water to see a glorious night sky and illuminating lights which reflected back upon the face of the water.

Facts

Common name: Common Roach
Scientific name: Rutilus rutilus
Status: Least concern
Size: Length 35-50cm

Adaptations
You will see, like most common species of fish, the common roach has dorsal and backside fins. They are a small fish, an adaptation that allows them to live in shallow waters. These roaches find food for survival. Like canadian geese fly together in a 'V' formation, roaches are extremely good at working together and regularly help each other to find food or warn of predators.

Habitat
This particular species of fish lives in areas such as regular, low land rivers and some large, turbid waters. I found the roach at Potteric Carr's Mother Drain.

Interdependence
The roach is an omnivore, because it eats plankton as well as smaller fish. A predator of the roach is the cormorant.

Did you know?
Roaches were first introduced in Ireland in the 1800's. They are currently one of the most prolific coarse fish.

Southern Hawker Dragonfly

The sun rises gloriously as I emerge from the reeds. I stretch my wings, and watch how the water shimmers. The sun beams down and brings everything to life. I fly around the pond like a guard waiting at the castle doors to warn off intruders.

I can feel the wind. Cold, crisp air brushes against my fragile wings. The sun beats down on my jewelled wings, making me glow. As I fly, I see all the green clumps of freshly cut grass, strewn across the wetland.

I notice a ruby red ladybird on a palmate leaf. I slowly swoop down and sneak up behind her. She starts to move. So I hover... once again, she stops. I immediately grab her in my powerful jaws and insert my pin-like teeth. Without mercy, I carry her away.

My crystal clear wings glide me away as I still grip my prey in my energetic jaw. I notice my home and I gradually lower myself. I land on the water's edge and devour my catch of the day.

Facts

Common name: Southern Hawker Dragonfly
Scientific name: Aeshna cyanea
Status: Least concern
Size: Wingspan 4-5cm. Length 7cmm.

Adaptations
You can spot a southern hawker dragonfly by their long, black bodies with green markings which are mostly oval in shape. If you look out for the males, they have little blue spots on their sides. Adult dragonflies use their wings to catch insects, taking them away to their offspring. They do this by flying straight into their prey, or sometimes, by killing their prey and carrying it back in their wings.

Habitat
You will often see the southern hawker dragonflies flying around near pond edges or rivers. At Potteric Carr, you can find then in Decoy Marsh. You will see them most often during the warmer months of June to September.

Interdependence
The southern hawker dragonfly is an omnivore and a tertiary consumer. They eat secondary consumers such as ladybirds, beetles and ants. The southern hawker dragonfly has a few predators, one being the newt. However, it usually gets away from its predators, because they can fly away from danger. As they get older, it takes them longer to get away. This means that they are more likely to get eaten as they get older.

Did you know?
The male southern hawker dragonflies crash into any intruders to scare them away and prevent attacks on other dragonflies and their offspring.

European Eel

As I swim with boldness, I feel my long tail wiggle within the cold refreshing water. My body feels so light and elegant. I see the darkness of the sky and the moon as an enormous light, shining gloriously on the lake. I hear the nocturnal creatures scurrying around. The water is very calm and motionless, and I can hear only faint noises as I swim around the quiet lake. Suddenly, I hear an air strike of rain approach me like an invading force.

As I swim in the murky water at the lake bed, I scavenge for prey. I see a pink, panicking worm trying to get back into the ground. I hide behind some weed like a hungry cheetah, sneaking up on his prey. I slowly move through the weeds performing a deadly dance. Quickening my pace from a snail to a torpedo, I strike like a bullet. Annihilating it like it is the last piece of food on the planet. It continues to panic, then I swallow it whole.

After I have eaten my exquisite worm, I meander off to some sharp, slippery rocks where I squeeze myself in for a superior sleep. As I start to fall asleep I see the mighty, burnt orange sun strike the lake, creating glamorous colours. I start to fall into a deep sleep. With my eyes still open, I see the rainbow-like pattern start to form on the lake.

I'm woken by splashing noises nearby. I start to hear them getting closer and closer and closer. I quickly rush out in a panic and look behind. I see nothing. I start to swim away feeling nervous then I see a black and yellow body coming closer and closer until...

Facts

Common name: European Eel
Scientific name: Anguilla anguilla
Status: Critically endangered
Size: Length 60-80cm. Weight 0.5-1.5 kg.

Adaptations
You can spot a European eel by their long and very slimy body and single pair of fins. The eel has a long ribbon-like fin going down almost the entire body. They have two main colours, dark green on the top and a darkish yellow on the bottom. Also, the European eel moves through the water by wiggling their tail from side-to-side.

Habitat
European eels live in all sorts of habitats like rivers, lakes and ponds. They mostly stay at the bottom of the water and sometimes come up to the surface at night, so you are most likely to see the european eel at night time. They sometimes hibernate in winter on the water bed.

Interdependence
The European eel feeds on insect larvae, molluscs, worms, and crustaceans. It is a secondary consumer and a carnivore. The European eel has no known predators.

Did you know?
European eel's migrate across most of the world.

Chub

I skim across the water's surface, watching with fear for the threat that I just escaped from. My group were just ambushed by a family of pike. We were no match. We only had one option. Swim. We managed to get away, but we were separated. I must keep moving, for all I know, the pike family could be right behind me. Right now, I have only one priority, food.

I feel an eerie silence. My swimming is silent. I'm trying to act calm but inside I'm panicking. I decide to hide in a rock, I hear something, something enormous. I'm hidden in a rock, hoping the pike won't find me. The king of the lake. He swims right past the rock, followed by the rest of his group. The smallest pike looks in the rock suspiciously. I thought he saw me for a second, but he is alerted to something away from the rock. I think they have found some food. My only chance.

I swim to the other side of the rock, deeper into the water, and away from the cold-blooded creatures. On the other side of the rock I have found a colony of water stick insects, I am grateful. Finally, food. I prey on them and move on. No time to waste. I see more movement in the distance and divert my direction, just in case. I swim into a mossy rock, a secure place to lay my eggs. If only my partner had survived to see the babies. If I paid more attention, he would have survived, but for now they lay there, waiting to hatch. The new generation.

Facts

Common name: Chub
Scientific name: Leuciscus cephalus
Status: Least concern
Size: Length 60-80cm

Adaptations
The chub is a cream and silver colour and have fairly big eyes with large gills on each side of the body. The chub fish has adapted to have multiple fins. The chub will tend to attack anything smaller than itself and will prey on the engaged creature. Anything bigger than the chub then it will consider it a threat and so will tend to stay away as it is not very lethal compared to other larger aquatic creatures.

Habitat
You will find that the chub fish tends to live in places like lakes, rivers, streams and ponds. This species of fish can be found in mostly freshwater and is fairly common in areas such as Decoy Marsh and Low Ellers Marsh.

Interdependence
Algae> insect larvae > chub > pike
This is a chub food chain. The algae is the producer, the one that generates energy for the food chain. Then you have the insect larvae as the primary consumer who eats the energy and nutrients from the producer. The chub is a secondary consumer and preys on insect larvae, small fish and fish eggs. The chub may be hunted by pike.

Did you know?
The chub is a fish that can be found anywhere from Canada to Europe and even the Arctic Circle.

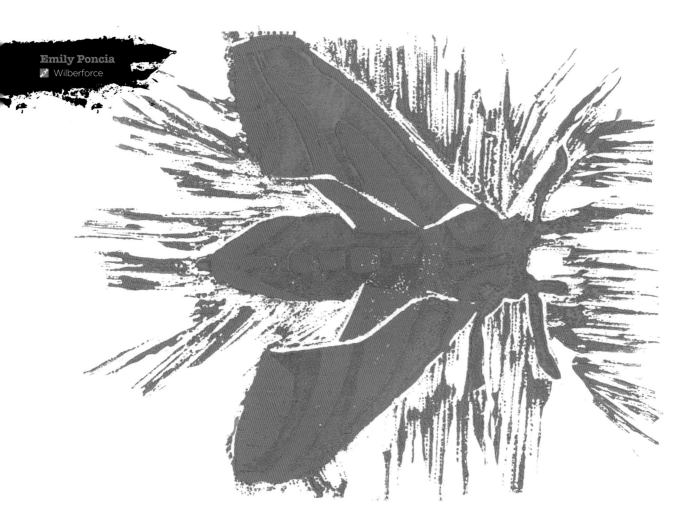

Elephant Hawk Moth

I wake from my deep, dreamy slumber, to the warmth of dusk. The setting sun brushes the landscape, creating a painting-like wash of pastel colours. Another evening. Another opportunity. I crawl into the thick rough grass which sways side to side to the music of the buzzing bees and singing birds. I begin another day at dusk; catching the last glimmers of sunlight. I am the elephant hawk moth and I am ready for what this day will bring!

I set off in a slow glide to make the most of the disappearing sunlight. I make sure to be alert and ready, in case there are any watchful bats or birds. As I fly across the vast meadow landscape, the evening air sweeps under my delicate wings. What a beautiful night! The setting sun slowly sinks below the horizon, illuminating the dense woods along the hillside in the distance. I can see budding fuchsia flowers, waiting to release their vivid colours into a pre-winter habitat. Their glowing hue tempts me. I keep flying.

Eventually, night draws to a close and the sun breaks through the trees, showing off mother nature's creation once again. The vibrant colours of the flora and the harmonised singing of the birds and insects leaks back into existence. As I slow, a multitude of colours fill my unsuspecting eyes. Sustenance. A fuchsia bursting with nectar. The pink stalks hang out holding a gift of satisfaction; sweet nectar. The sweetness overflows my senses: the taste, the smell, the texture. I silently go from fuchsia to fuchsia, in a grove of colour.

Facts

Common name: Elephant Hawk Moth
Scientific name: Deilephila elpenor
Status: Least concern
Size: Wingspan 50-70mm.

Adaptations
You can spot the larvae by the section on their head that looks like a elephant trunk, which extends and retracts as a defense system. Its body inflates making the four eye markings look bigger. Larvae go through metamorphosis to become an adult elephant hawk moth. You can identify the adults by their exotic green and pink colours. Their eyes are non-reflective so they have an increased ability to see in low light and are not easily detected in moonlight by other animals. They come out at night so they are not caught by day birds.

Habitat
You can find the species in habitats including farmland, grassland, clearings, meadows and woodlands. At Potteric Carr you might find them at Loversall Field. Adults can be found from May until early August.

Interdependence
The elephant hawk moth is a herbivore and is a primary consumer. They eat producers such as roots and leaves and the nectar from plants such as honeysuckles. They are particularly fond of fuchsias. They are sometimes eaten by day birds but more commonly bats. The larvae can be mistaken for a snake so that usually puts possible predators off.

Did you know?
The elephant hawk moth gets the name because the larvae are long and look similar to the trunk of an elephant.

Pike

As I was awoken by the cool, crisp current, angelically drifting over my scaly skin, my translucent fins like a silk cloth, I suddenly realise I am not alone. I need to make the decision. Life or death? Attack or hide?

Through the murky water, I see a stickleback, searching for its prey. Unknown, defenceless to my mighty wrath, I strike. In an instant, the lifeless body is draped over my lower jaw, my once green scales now blood red. As half of the lifeless body drifts down, I think to myself, I am finally satisfied.

Yet, I am still not alone down here in the murky depths. I see nothing but mud. I think to myself it is not worth the risk of injury. I'm full, I got what I came for. I swim away with all my strength. Back to my family, where I'm safe at last.

Facts

Common name: Pike
Scientific name: Esox lucius
Status: Least concern
Size: Length 147cm

Adaptations
The pike is perfectly streamlined. It has a long, slender body and forked tail, which allows it move quickly to catch its prey or swim away, if threatened. The pike has a dark olive green colour with yellowish spots which camouflage it against the lake bed, so its prey can't see it. It has a large, strong jaw with big teeth to clamp down on its prey, when hunting. The pike often makes its translucent fins flare up to attract a mate.

Habitat
The pike lives in deep, murky water. You'll find it during warm weather, in the fresh water streams at Potteric Carr. Little is known about its night time behaviors.

Interdependence
A pike is dependent on perch and is a tertiary consumer. It is not an apex predator. It is hunted by the osprey, but thanks to the pike's speed and agility, it often gets away.

Did you know?
Did you know that the pike has translucent fins, which means that they are partially see through?

Common Damsel Bug

As I sit on a leaf watching the serene surroundings of the trees and blades of grass, the rain hammers down on the damp ground below. The water droplets are like many knives falling down to earth, stabbing my back with a cold, wet bite. My leaf mattress makes a comfortable resting place, while I wait until meal time.

The damp air clings to my body as I fly through the woods, trying to find some food. The malodorous scent of the damp trees penetrates my body, leaving a taste of unpleasantness. I can see the restless twigs and leaves rustling in the howling wind.

As I am flying through the woods, I spot a small caterpillar perched on the branch of a nearby tree. I fly down and land in a place not far from the caterpillar, I decide to move in on the unsuspecting prey. Waiting for the feast to begin, I edge closer and closer until... bang! I pounce! Sinking my beak into its body. The caterpillar supplies me with a nutritious meal.

As I fly back to my safe haven, the rain starts to calm and I become sleepy. When I return to my leaf mattress I burrow down and I allow myself to fall asleep, forgetting about the rain around me.

Facts

Common name: Common Damsel Bug
Scientific name: Nabis rugosus
Status: Least concern
Size: Length 8-12cm

Adaptations
The common damsel bug's anatomical adaptations include its wings to help it fly, as well as its beak, which it uses to suck the insides out of its prey after catching them. Another anatomical adaptation is its long front legs to catch and hold its prey.

Habitat
You can find the common damsel bug on the edge of woods and grasslands. If you visit Potteric Carr, you might find it in Beeston Plantation or in the wood around Willow or Decoy Marshes.

Interdependence
The common damsel will eat insects smaller than itself such as the caterpillar. The common damsel bug is a secondary consumer. It is an omnivore meaning it eats animals and plants.

Did you know?
Damsel bugs can act as natural pest control for crops by eating the insects that can harm plants.

Common Frog

Previously deserted, the pond comes to life in an array of beautiful, vibrant colours. The gentle breeze blows over the pond, tenderly skipping over the murky, brown water. The orange sun rises into the sky, changing it to a vivid blue, a display of pink and orange, illuminating the clouds. I lay there staring, as if hypnotised, on my usual rock, relaxing, lazily. I observe animals by the pond, crawling out of their shelters into the clearing, searching for food. I jump from my rock, keeping an eye out for a victim to feast on. I spot a fly speeding round, too close to the ground. I wait for an opportunity and concentrate my aim on the target, focusing relentlessly. I release my long sticky tongue, hitting my target with accuracy, quickly pulling it back into my mouth. I repeat this until I'm full, satiated, all hunger gone.

As I lazily hop back to my nest... wait, what was that? My senses alerted by the sound of a bird in the distance. The sound was familiar, exactly like the one I'd heard the day before, although this time, it sounded hungry. It was after me. Scared, I hide in the nearest bush. The bird, that I suspect is a hawk, circles, searching with its powerful vision. The bird sees a stray frog, oblivious to its own danger, near the pond and dives with pinpoint accuracy, striking its target with precision. I retreat further into the bush, shocked by the horrendous scene. I sneak too far back and fall straight into the hawk's vision, it notices me immediately. I awaited my inevitable fate. However, to my surprise the hawk was distracted by an even bigger meal. I jumped away as fast as possible, petrified with fear, into the thick foliage until I am hidden from view.

Facts

Common name: Common Frog
Scientific name: Rana temporaria
Status: Least concern
Size: Length 6-9cm. Weight 22.7g.

Adaptations
One of the common frog's many adaptations is their long sticky tongue to catch flies in mid air. This helps them when hunting so they don't have to move that much to catch the prey; so barely any energy is used. Common frogs have a lot more adaptations, such as the ability to breathe through their skin, which enables them to hibernate for the coming months under leaves and mud piles. They can breathe through their lungs, depending on the surroundings. They also have transparent inner eyelids, which means they can protect their eyes under water. They also have the ability to change their skin colour according to the environment, and live both underwater and above the surface. They can absorb water through their skin so they do not need to drink.

Habitat
The common frog generally lives near, and in ponds, as well as wetlands and grasslands. These areas are the usual places for a frog to live because of the dampness. This helps to keep their skin moist so they don't become dehydrated.

Interdependence
The common frog is a secondary consumer and lives on a diet of insects, such as flies. The primary consumer, in this example, is a fly which eats the producer (detritus).

Did you know?
Common frogs eat, on average, 15 flies a day.

Water Scorpion

Sunbeams dazzle, reflecting off the rippling surface of the lake. I wake from a good night's sleep upon the long reed bed. The reeds rustle as the painful wind rushes past me. I spot my prey, the water spider. I stay still and silent, rooted to the spot. It sees me, but it is too late. I jump out at it. I eat it. Gripping the spider with my needle-like pincers, I inject it with deadly digestive enzymes. After my snack, I disappear out of the rippled water, onto the grass.

The tall green blades of grass tower above me. The sensation of the birds tweeting in song overloads me with beautiful sounds. I hear a quiet murmur from the reeds, I am alert to danger. I scan carefully, but there is nothing in my vision except a dirty frog. I check again. There is nothing.

My tiny hairs detect the vibration of a loud noise from the sky, like a group of children running down the stairs. I see clouds turning into a wall of grey. I hastily retreat home before the 'bombing' rain starts.

As I enter the water, my predator, a carp, spots me, The gorgeous but deadly colour of the carp shining, it charges at me. I hide instantaneously. I think it has gone. I try to see if it has gone... I can still see it! I am terrified. It comes at me one last time, getting closer and closer.

Facts

Common name: Water Scorpion
Scientific name: Nepidae
Status: Least concern
Size: Length 30mm. Width 30mm.

Adaptations
You can spot a water scorpion by the brown shades on its back, and the distinctive pincers at the front of the body. Water scorpions are mainly found at the bottom ponds. When they swim the tail becomes vertical, so that no predators can strike them from behind. You will struggle to hear the water scorpion swimming because they are silent, meaning predators or prey can't hear them.

Habitat
You can find water scorpions in deep ponds and reeds. At Potteric Carr, you might see them at Willow Marsh, though the reeds make it hard for you to find them. You mainly see them between April and August.

Interdependence
The water scorpion is an omnivore and a predator. It eats secondary consumers such as water worms. It also eats producers like reeds. The water scorpion has few predators, but occasionally, it is eaten by carp and birds, such as blackbirds and magpies. It is very aggressive towards both predators and prey.

Did you know?
Water scorpions breath with their tail. They have little holes that take air from the water.

Grass Snake

I wake up one morning in the peaceful, warm weather, looking around, regarding the rough terrain. I lay on the damp, slimy floor, noticing that an oak tree has fallen into my trench.

While I'm slithering and twisting my body, I ascend up the slimy, damp wall. Now I'm out. I catch the scent of the fresh air. The dirt beneath me touches my soft underbelly and the warmth from the sun above warms my scales. I cannot linger, I must begin my search for food.

I scavenge for many juicy and delicious animals, but my favourite is the vole. I hunt for hours and hours, looking for any food I like, but I have no luck. However, on my return, I glimpse a vole wandering around. I decide to strike. I slither over to the vole. I pounce and bite, devouring my prey slowly. I'm full and satisfied. I'm going back home to sleep and digest my food.

Facts

Common name: Grass Snake
Scientific name: Natrix natrix
Status: Least concern
Size: Length 70-100cm. Weight 240g.

Adaptations
You can seen them with stripes and spots used for camouflage. With no legs, arms, ears or other appendages, the grass snake can slither through grass or among rocks without causing the prey to get frightened. Grass snakes have lost their venom through evolution. Grass snakes are great swimmers. They are fast-moving animals. The grass snake is defensive and will protect itself and its young. The grass snakes will not attack if it is not hunting you, or, if you have not provoked it.

Habitat
You can find grass snakes in rough land pastures, woodland, wet heathlands, gardens, parks and hedgerows. You can find grass snakes at Decoy Marsh and Willow Marsh, in the twig piles and sun traps made by the staff at Potteric Carr. They are mostly found in the woods and trenches around and inside Potteric Carr.

Interdependence
The grass snake's predators are storks, owls, sparrow hawks, foxes and domestic cats. A grass snake is a carnivore and a secondary consumer. Grass snakes eat mostly amphibians, such as the common toad/frog, although they will eat voles and, sometimes, ants.

Did you know?
Grass snakes molt once a year. The skin will be removed in one piece. The grass snake is fragile and aggressive during this period.

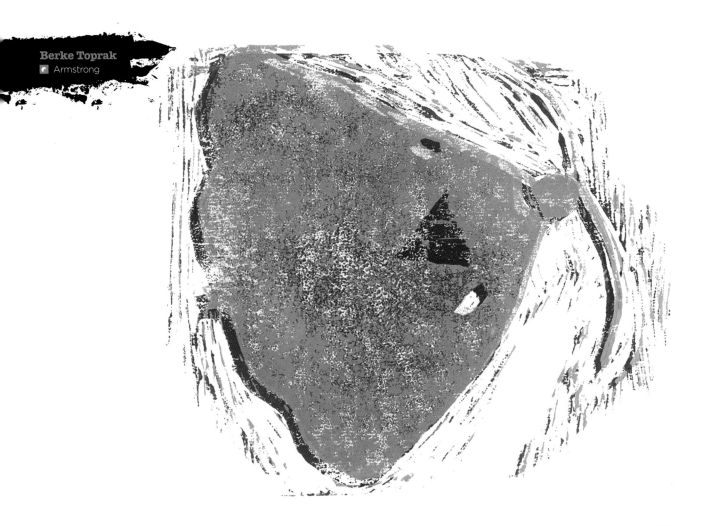

Silver Y

The farm, the fresh air, the sun burns the warm corn. My home is warm, the birds tweet and squeak. I safely make my way to the berries. Enjoying the fresh juicy berries, the birds spot me. I make my way back. Away from danger, I fly over the flowers. They smell sweet and fragrant, they smell good. I take a break and have a little taste.

After my delicious lunch, I go to my home and take a rest. After taking a six hour nap, I take my breakfast and, again, my lunch. After my days are over, I get old, I die. I rest in my place. I go on, dead forever, I've left my five eggs. Once they hatch, there will be more silver Ys.

Facts

Common name: Silver Y
Scientific name: Autographa gamma
Status: Least concern
Size: Wingspan 30-45mm

Adaptations
The silver Y has wings shaped like a Y. You can identify them because of the shades of brown and grey on their wings. This camouflages them in their habitat. They like to fly at night, or, in the day when it is overcast. The silver Y has an adaptation of growing wings. This happens when it's at its next stage of becoming a moth. It uses its wings to fly and its legs to move. It lays 1-5 eggs. The eggs are hidden on the surface of leaves.

Habitat
You can see the silver Y living in open areas like farms, woodlands or grassland such as Willow Marsh at Potteric Carr.

Interdependence
It is a garden/farm species. It can be found in crops and eating flowers, which it sees when it is flying over crops.

Did you know?
The silver Y can produce 2 or 3 generations of offspring in a year.

Leafhopper

I awake from the shiny, sharp holly leaf in which I have immersed myself in during the chilly night. I see the towering blades of emerald green grass, standing firm like a castle wall. This is my realm. The dew drops hang elegantly like crystals on a chandelier. I see the ruby red ladybirds, sat happily on a shiny leaf, quenching their thirst with dew droplets.

Hopping cautiously from leaf to leaf, I avoid the danger of getting drowned by some of the colossal droplets that are invading my realm. My luminous body stands out like a lighthouse in the dark night, amongst this emerald green grass. I quickly assert myself and leap eagerly towards the multicoloured outcrop of spring flowers. Now, happily camouflaged in the wondrous colour surrounding, I go in search of my delicacy, tree sap.

Within fifty leaps, I have found my nourishment. Burrowing through the dry, weak bark, I place my piercing, sucking mouth upon the sap, finally getting my fill of glorious golden liquid.

Facts

Common name: Leafhopper
Scientific name: Cicadellidae
Status: High concern
Size: Length 2-15mm

Adaptations
The leafhopper has four wings so that they are able to jump further. This is an example of an anatomical adaptation. The most common species of leafhopper at Potteric Carr is coloured green to help it blend in with its environment – also an anatomical adaptation. The leafhopper has two big, strong back legs, so that it can jump further. One of its behavioural adaptations is that it can burrow into a tree and suck out honeydew to feed on.

Habitat
You will find the leafhoppers on tree leaves or in a patch of clover. They are very shy and will quickly hop away if noise is made. The leafhopper only comes out in warm temperatures, 15ºC or higher. You will find them around marsh land, such as the Willow Marsh area of Potteric Carr. However, you won't find them in water. They would drown because they haven't got the right adaptations for swimming.

Interdependence
The leafhopper is a primary consumer and lives mainly on a diet of tree sap. The leafhopper can fall prey to red ants which are secondary consumers.

Did you know?
Leafhoppers have actually been seen feeding honeydew to geckos, which are a type of lizard!

Smooth Newt

It's a hot summer's day when the sun is at its highest. The warmth of the sun hits me rapidly, as I slowly creep out of my den. The calm, swaying water wakes me. My body drifts at the bottom of the pond. I glide through my homeland, looking for my prey. Waiting, until I spot what I am looking for. My prey is up ahead. As I slowly float across, my prey moves. I freeze. I don't move, until it turns back around. I am disguised by my surroundings, not moving a muscle in my body. Finally, it turns away. I make my move. I pounce on my prey, not giving it an inch. I scramble to my den, carrying my prey with me. I divide my prey into two, eating it slowly, enjoying the luxurious sensation in my mouth. It tastes divine. It's gone in an instant. The tadpole doesn't live to see another day.

Surrounded by tall umbrella-like trees, that almost touch the sky like fingers reaching into the air, I explore for food. Now the breeding season is over, I travel far and wide searching for sustenance. The trees tower above me, waving in the air. The trunks of the trees have deep, dark holes in, that you can almost see through. Spiky thorn bushes tangle around the base of their trunks, weaving in and out of the holes in the twisted timber. Above the trees there are large, puffy marshmallow-like clouds, with the scorching sun lighting up the sky. As the day comes to an end, I finish my last snack and hurry back to my den, where I rest for another night.

Facts

Common name: Smooth Newt
Scientific name: Lissotriton vulgaris
Status: Least concern
Size: Length 10 cm approx

Adaptations
You can identify smooth newts by the light brown or olive green colour on their bodies. They have small dark spots on their throats. Females and males both have orange coloured bellies, covered with small black spots. Females can be identified by their body colour, which is paler than the male. On land, you'll find the newt catching prey by sticking their tongue out, but in water they simply hunt using their teeth.

Habitat
Newts are most commonly encountered in ponds. You can find them at Potteric Carr in the wildlife pond in the marsh land. Smooth newts can be found in a variety of habitats outside of the breeding season. They are the largest and rarest newts found in Britain.

Interdependence
The smooth newt survives on slugs, fish, other newts, water lice, water shrimps, water fleas, worms and other small insects. The smooth newt is a carnivore, because it eats other animals. It is a secondary consumer. It is preyed on by thrushes and other birds.

Did you know?
Smooth newts shed their skin almost twice a week. Newts can regenerate severed tails, digits, or even complete limbs. They also have the ability to extract oxygen from water.

Banded Demoiselle

The sun rose behind the dark, grey clouds. My eyes opened to the landscape in front of me. The pond lay motionless. Sun peeked through any gaps it could find, trying desperately to break through. Reeds surrounded me, swaying gently. No visitors were around yet, and most insects and animals were still sleeping. I stared at the landscape. It made me feel so awkward, so unwanted and so misplaced. The view in front of me was soon dull and boring, nothing but greyness and stillness enveloping me.

I was about to glide up into the sky, like a marvellous ice skater stepping onto ice, when a splash of water jumped into the air. I hesitated. All was still again. All of a sudden, a green beast clambered out of the water and pounced on me. My wings flapped frantically and I flew away as fast as a finely tuned racing car. I landed again, a little further down the pond. The clouds shifted and the sun broke through. The world had been given colour again, and it looked beautiful.

My tummy rumbled and yelled to be filled with breakfast. The pond was still motionless. However, there was now a rainbow of colours, erupting from the reflection of the sun on the water. I flew up into the air with my three pairs of legs dangling down. They act as a net. A fly flew into it, and in an instance, it was doomed. I landed and dug my teeth into its flesh. As I looked up, a beautiful, emerald female demoiselle darted past. I decided to follow it, performing an aerial dance.

Facts

Common name: Banded Demoiselle (Damselfly)
Scientific name: Calopteryx splendens
Status: Least concern
Size: Wingspan (hindwing) 36mm. Length 45mm.

Adaptations
You will spot a male banded demoiselle if you look for their electric blue body and huge black eyes. Males also have blue wings, with a black circle in the centre. You can spot a female if you look for their lime green body and wings. They might be hard to spot, as they can travel at 100 times their own body length, per second. Another adaptation is that their flight is 'fluttering' and butterfly-like. To attract females and entice them into their territories, males lift their wings, performing an aerial dance and a dazzling display of flight.

Habitat
You can usually find them near slow, lowland rivers and streams, especially those with muddy bottoms. You may find them near Decoy Lake at Potteric Carr, as there is a lot of grass and reeds around a shallow river lake. Their flight period is during the summer months from May to August.

Interdependence
The banded demoiselle is an omnivore and is a primary consumer. It eats producers such as plants. Its predators are frogs.

Did you know?
Dragonflies have the best eyesight in the world. They have compound eye sight. Each eye is made up of 30,000 cells, known as ommatidia.

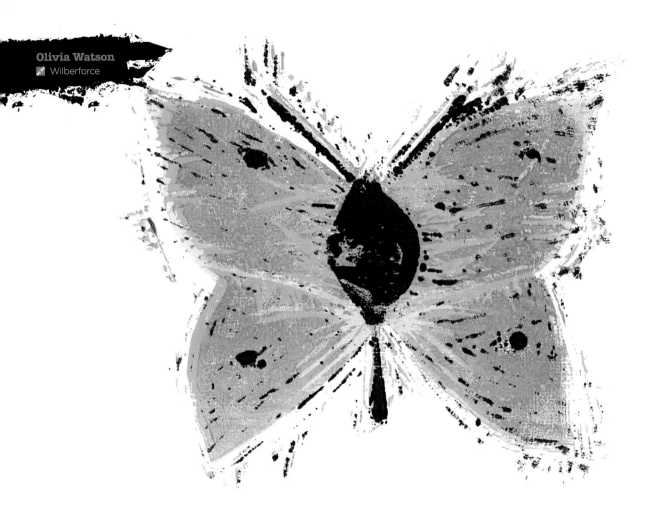

Brimstone Butterfly

I emerge from my chrysalis in late July, as the sun reflects on the murky, bug-infested water. I notice the small ripples moving on the water surface as if they are swimming. Other butterflies gracefully float past me, leaving the area in a range of different colours.

Birds, hidden in the trees, acting as if they aren't even there, sing to the sunrise. I hear the heavy gusts of the wind, forcing itself through the giant wood. The air is smothered in the delightful smell of freshly cut, green grass which lays untouched on the hard floor.

As I land on a bright flower hidden behind thick trees, I can feel the gentle petals that rest beneath my colourful body. They are delicately swaying as the soft wind carefully brushes through the gaps in the flower. I am suddenly alarmed. I am being pushed by a stronger butterfly who's trying to take my flower. I grip on with all of my strength. It eventually gives up and leaves.

I lay undisturbed on the delicate flower, feeding on the yellow nectar as I rest.

Facts

Common name: Brimstone Butterfly
Scientific name: Gonepteryx rhamni
Status: Least concern
Size: Wingspan 60mm

Adaptations
You can spot the brimstone from its bright yellow and green wings. If you look carefully, female brimstone butterflies have lighter green wings whereas the males have green and yellow wings. Also the under wing of a brimstone butterfly is a leafy camouflage for when hibernating or hunting.

Habitat
Brimstone adults emerge from their chrysalis in May and July. They hibernate over the winter in woodlands and are found around areas of water such as ponds. You can find them around Willow Marsh at Potteric Carr. You are also most likely to see them in August.

Interdependence
The brimstone butterfly is a herbivore. Its diet is nectar, rotting fruit, pollen and animal dung. It has predators including birds such as the robin. It is part of a food chain, e.g. autumn gentian > brimstone > robin > sparrowhawk. This means the brimstone butterfly is the primary consumer.

Did you know?
The brimstone butterfly's life span is only 12-13 months.

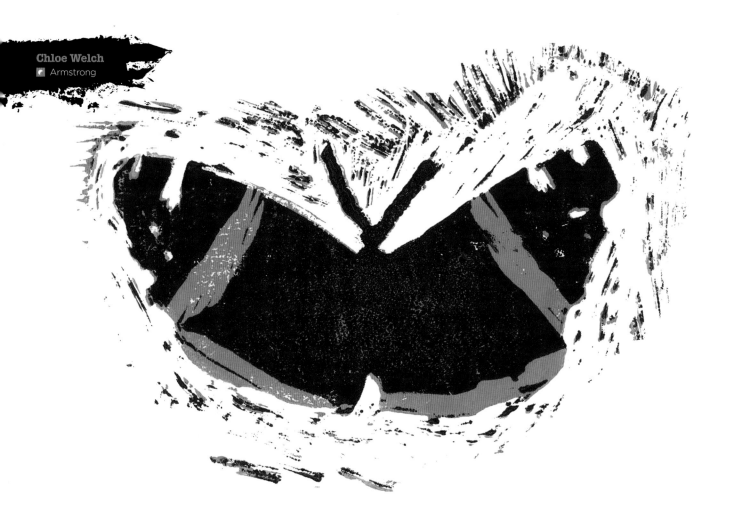

Red Admiral Butterfly

The beautiful colours of the flowers started to hit me all at once, like a diamond shimmering and shining in the sun. I flit from place to place, not having an obvious home, from towns to mountains.

As I flutter across the lavish meadows, the scent of fresh air rushes towards me. There's smells I have never encountered before. The pollen of the flowers start to draw me in, closer and closer, like a child in a sweet shop.

My antenna feels for the touch of the cushion-like meadows below my elegant wings. I sense my predators flying nearer and nearer, knowing that at any second, a robin could come and devour me with one gulp, like a guard dog on watch.

The day draws to a close. My wings start to feel heavy, like I have the world resting on my shoulders. As I try to find a stable home for night, the nocturnal animals come out to play. I see a bramble bush from the corner of my eye. My home for the night.

Facts

Common name: Red Admiral Butterfly
Scientific name: Vanessa atalanta
Status: Least concern
Size: Wingspan 67-72mm. Length 35mm. Weight 20g.

Adaptations
You can spot the red admiral due to its striking orange, white and black patterns that stand out. The butterfly feels for the touch of pollen with their antenae. They fly alone or in pairs during mating season. The lifespan of a red admiral butterfly is usually 10 months, which is a good age for a butterfly.

Habitat
The red admiral is usually found in meadows and woodlands. At Potteric Carr, for example, you'll encounter them in Loversall Field. It is a diurnal animal, meaning it only comes out in the day time. It sleeps at night. The red admiral is also known to hibernate in winter.

Interdependence
The red admiral is a herbivore. and a primary consumer that eats producers, such as rotting fruits and pollen from flowers. The red admiral has a few predators, including birds such as robins.

Did you know?
The red admiral's favourite food is a nettle. If it can't locate nettles, they try to find rotting fruit and flower pollen.

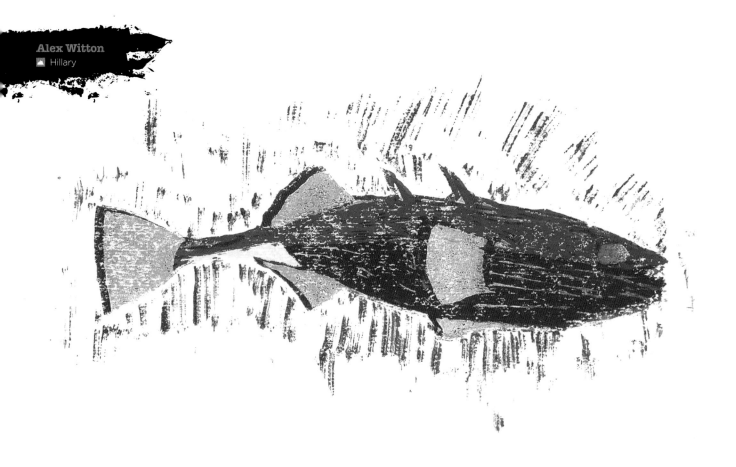

Stickleback

The sunrise cut into the water like a dagger. The colours bursting into the sky, like fireworks. The water gently rippled in an angelic rhythm and the pearlescent shells shimmered against the sand, like gold. The green weeds were grabbing at everything, like lost souls, and the water was a clear blue. The reflection of the green trees gave the lake an emerald tint. The waters were calm.

Then, the shoal quickly went into hiding as a malevolent, putrid, pike emerged from the scrawny weeds, gliding whilst scanning the perimeter of our territory. The pike locked onto its target. Its soulless eyes glaring into me. It started hurtling towards us at the speed of a torpedo. We started our tit-for-tat strategy. The first fish struck. He darted forward and back, making sure to bite a deep chunk of flesh out of the pike's scaly skin. Our first success. We got ready to make another attack. The next fish replicated the move, and the next and the next, making sure to dodge any of the pike's strikes. The sticklebacks darted about frantically in terror, but nevertheless, remained determined. The blood stained pike, glistening red, gave up in pain and bolted off as quick as he could, before we launched another attack.

The water was clear except for where our battle had taken place. The water had gone a murky, brown and scarlet colour because the sand and blood had mixed with the water. It looked like a sandstorm.

The battle had given the neighbourhood a shock. Fear had filled our eyes at that terrible moment.

Facts

Common name: Stickleback
Scientific name: Gasterosteidae
Status: Least concern
Size: Length 4-7cm. Weight 1g.

Adaptations

In the spring mating season, the male stickleback gets a bright red throat and belly, and does a mating dance to attract a female. The female can lay up to 400 eggs. The male looks after them and teaches them to defend themselves until they are mature enough to leave. Sticklebacks have 2-10 spikes on their back. If a predator tries to eat one, the spikes make it almost impossible. They spit them out, giving it another chance to live.

Habitat

You will be able to find sticklebacks in wetlands, lakes, rivers, streams, ponds and occasionally in the sea. You will find them at Potteric Carr in Mother Drain and Decoy Marsh.

Interdependence

You will see them eating water insect larvae, water fleas, worms, snails, fish eggs, tadpoles and land insects that have fallen into the water. The energy moves up through the food chain, ie, the tadpole eats the algae, the stickleback eats the tadpole and so on. If a disease wiped out the stickleback, the food chain would collapse because the species are all dependent on each other. This is called interdependence. The stickleback is a carnivore because they eat other creatures.

Did you know?

The male attracts females by building a nest of waterweed, detritus and algae. He makes it with his mouth, which creates a small dome or bower.

Common Newt

The wind blew through the waving, tall trees towards the undulating water, making rushing ripples and helping to push the rustling leaves down the river rapids.

I, the brown, silver and green newt, popped out of a nearby rustling bush. I had just woken from my slumber and I was hungry for some glorious food. Worms and snails are my prime targets around the wet grassland, but today I fancy an underwater animal. Maybe tadpoles? I slithered stealthily through to the river, using the rustling leaves as a bridge towards the most convenient spot to enter. I made the plunge, like a shark determined to catch a seal.

As I swam through the dismal depths, I scanned my immediate environment, using my aquatic vision to pinpoint a tadpole feast. I checked that the coast was clear of predators, then sped like a bullet towards them. The green murky water almost obscured the tadpoles, but I kept them in sight until I was in striking position. I attacked. None escaped.

As I clambered out of water, I was satisfied. Then, suddenly, I noticed something. A twitch in the bushes. I wondered, prey or predator? Run or fight? I decided to stay and fight it out. It came as suddenly as a flashback, striking mercilessly. My fate had been decided. I was lost.

Facts

Common name: Common Newt
Scientific name: Lissotriton vulgaris
Status: Least concern
Size: Length 10cm approx

Adaptations
Common newts have long streamlined bodies which helps them move through water. They have dark skin for camouflage from predators and sneaking up on their prey. Newts have the incredible ability to grow back body parts including organs, limbs and upper and lower jaws if they lose them or they are damaged by a predator. The common newt can produce a toxin to protect itself from predators. The female newt lays eggs and does not give birth to young. Newts are not aggressive in nature. They are nocturnal in their usual habitat, and sometimes, they hibernate at the bottom of a pond.

Habitat
Nowadays, you are most likely to see a common newt in a garden pond. At Potteric Carr, you will find them in pools and ponds around the reserve during the spring. It hunts on land and water and, usually, it eats slugs or worms.

Interdependence
Living plants support the whole of this food chain. In food chains, the animals need to stay in balance or the whole food chain would start to decrease in numbers, towards extinction. The common newt is in the third trophic level and is a carnivore.

Did you know?
The newt can breath through its skin, so it doesn't have to open its mouth in water to risk choking. It can breathe in air too, using its lungs.

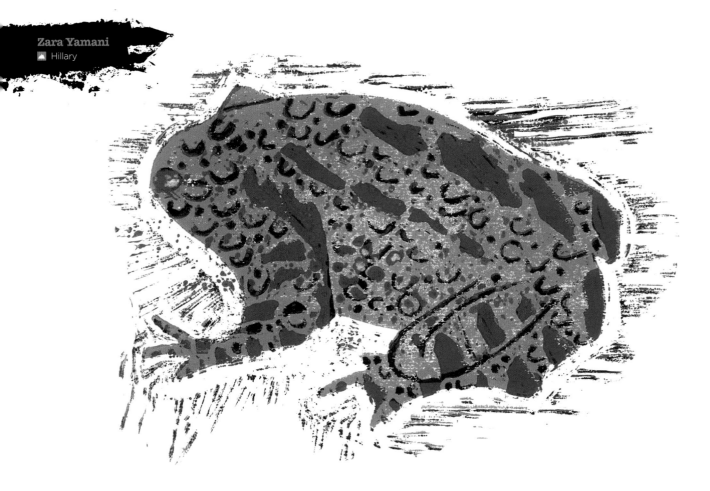

Common Toad

I open my eyes. Through the leafy roof of my burrow I can see thousands of stars glimmering like crystals in the velvety black of the night, whilst the cratered crust of the moon illuminates my wooded surroundings. A gentle summer breeze greets me as I crawl out into the darkness, where my acute night vision makes out the gloomy silhouettes of the tall trees, which lean against each other like frail, fragile old men, reaching towards the heavens with their long, spindly fingers.

As I crawl along, I can feel the dry, crunchy leaves crackling beneath me; although, thankfully, my green-tinted skin is well camouflaged against the vivid forest carpet. However, I soon spot something that has not been quite so lucky. It is an Orange Banded Arion Slug, leaving a glistening silvery trail as it makes its way through the undergrowth. My hunting instinct takes over as I edge towards my prey. Soon, I am so close that I could reach out and touch it, but the slug obliviously continues on its journey. Now the moment is right. My tongue shoots out. The sticky fibres ensnare the slug. All that remains is a ghostly trail, which ends abruptly, with no warning; another reminder of the brutality of nature. I cannot help but notice that the stars are getting lighter, like drawings on a piece of paper after having being dipped into water. I feel a sense of calm as the sky is painted into a fiery watercolour; pinks, purples, reds and oranges set my world alight. Reality gradually fades into dreams, as I fall asleep to the lullaby of nature.

Facts

Common name: Common Toad
Scientific name: Bufo bufo
Status: Least concern
Size: Width 5-7cm. Length 8-13cm. Weight 20-30g.

Adaptations
The common toad has many surprising adaptations. It has dry, warty skin to camouflage it with the dry woodland leaves. It also has a long, sticky tongue to help it catch its prey and webbed feet to help it move in water. The common toad can secrete poisonous toxins from behind its eyelids, making it distasteful to predators. However, it would be difficult to get close enough to see this, as they have the incredible ability to change colour to match environmental conditions such as soil colour.

Habitat
The common toad is nocturnal so you are most likely to find them in woodland, grassland and scrub at night-time. During the winter, you would be unlikely to see a common toad as they hibernate, normally under logs, plant pots or similar damp hiding places. If you want to see one at Potteric Carr, the best places to look would be Corbett Wood and Corbett Field.

Interdependence
The rough grass is a producer which is eaten by the herbivorous orange banded arion slug (a consumer) . When the carnivorous common toad (a consumer) eats the slug, the slugs energy is passed on to the toad. The toad, however, is then eaten by the carnivorous grass snake (a consumer).

Did you know?
Common toads have such a good sense of smell that they know when earthquakes are going to happen just by smelling the chemical changes in the air!